Dr. Marny Hall

THE LAVENDER COUCH

A Consumer's Guide to Psychotherapy for Lesbians and Gay Men

Boston · Alyson Publications, Inc.

This is a paperback original from Alyson Publications, Inc., PO Box 2783, Boston, MA 02208. Distributed in England by Gay Men's Press, PO Box 247, London, N15 6RW.

First edition, March 1985   5 4 3 2 1

ISBN 0 932870 41 4

Contents

Breakthrough

You tell me that I am on a journey,
an odyssey.
You tell me that it will be months
before I am home again.
I have tried to prepare for this.
I have left my job.
I have almost stopped smoking.
I have taken to vegetables,
and yoga
and sometimes I even throw the I Ching.
But somehow this is not enough.
There is a place in my body
which has become displaced.
Lost.
I am struggling to find it.
I am not sure if all this
is called a break-down.

I am much too afraid to ask.
So, I imagine, and sometimes
I feel like Alice falling through
the looking glass.
I do not know when all this
will end.
You say it will be months.
And I believe you.
Because this is how I came to you,
a proud woman,
who never asked for many things
not even from old lovers.
I came to you
and asked for everything.
This is the moment
where bones can crack
like eggshells.
You choose to say
we are both going
on this journey together.
Someday, I will show you
the hills
in which I used to stamp my feet
and dance.
Today, it is enough to hear
my friends say
that I am looking better.

1977

Willyce Kim

Acknowledgements

The encouragement of my friends and colleagues throughout the process of producing this book was precious to me.

Marcy Adelman, Meredith Maran, Anne Larson, Debigail Mazor, Lauree Moss and Diana E.H. Russell advised and counseled me, offered feedback and new ideas, wept and rejoiced with me during critical junctures in the process. My gratitude and love to each of them.

I want to thank the members of OPTIONS: AN INSTITUTE FOR LIFESTYLE EDUCATION — Joanne Gardner-Loulan, Arthur Atlas, Jack Morin and Jan Zobel — for some of the formulations in the book. Their willingness to read the manuscript along the way, point out blind spots, and suggest new directions is very much appreciated.

Charles Silverstein and Ann Heron served as my distant muses. The time each of them took with the manuscript helped to balance my California biases with some East Coast perspective.

The ground-breaking work done by Betty Berzon and Don Clark in the area of lesbian-and-gay-affirmative therapy has influenced me profoundly. It is on their theoretical foundation that this book was built. I also relied heavily upon Jonathan Katz' meticulous research in articulating my historical perspective.

A central goal of this book was to demonstrate how client empowerment can be transformed into consumer action. Bill Cliadakis, Gary Schoener and John Grace have been concerned with the practical applications of clients' rights for years and they generously shared their ideas and resources with me. I am grateful to them for their guidance in this area.

I am particularly indebted to Freda Krumholz for her expert technical assistance. After glimpsing my stapled, pasted, spindled and mutilated first draft, Freda shut her ears to my protests and dragged me to a computer fair. She oversaw the purchase of my word-processor and provided me with ongoing moral and technical support. She has been extremely generous with her time and expertise.

My brother, Richard Hall, has been a wonderful source of comfort and encouragement throughout the writing process. His editorial suggestions, as well as his wisdom and experience in the areas of writing and publishing, have been invaluable to me.

Meredith Maran never ceased to dazzle me with her organizational talent and editorial acumen. No future sentence I write will be complete unless it bristles with her distinctive cross-outs and crisply printed insertions. Her contribution to the book is immeasurable.

From the inception of this project, I have felt tremendously supported by Sasha Alyson. His support buoyed me through the hardest times and I am more grateful to him than I can say.

Finally, I want to thank the lesbians and gay men who shared with me their experience both as clients and counselors. Their stories are the heart of the book.

To the girl from Travis County

Introduction

by Charles Silverstein, Ph.D.

This is a unique book. It's the first one prepared for gay
people to guide them in the choice of a therapist, with
sound advice on how to evaluate their therapeutic experience. You'll find an enormous number of vignettes, short
stories of the good and bad experiences that lesbians and
gay men have had with both good therapists, and those
not so good. I may as well add my own.

At the age of sixteen (it was 1950) I was in turmoil.
Beyond the usual chaos present in most adolescent boys, I
had the additional problem of knowing — that is to say,
believing — I was infected with that toxin called "homosexuality." There was no place to turn. I certainly wasn't
going to talk to my parents; I never discussed personal
things with them. I knew no gay people. So I decided to
read about it. It seemed like a good thing to do.

Across the street from my high school was a small library that sat next to a storefront church. The church had a

large clock, over which was a sign that said, "It is time to seek the Lord." For the next few weeks, during my lunch hour, I walked to that library (carefully avoiding looking at the clock) and read everything available on the subject of homosexuality. What a disaster! I was sicker than I ever knew.

I rushed to my family doctor and confessed my illness. He immediately took out his prescription pad and wrote out the name of the local mental health clinic, handed it to me and ushered me out of his office (he didn't even charge me). I called, probably from a pay phone, made an appointment and showed up at the clinic ready to be cured. It's amazing how well I can remember that clinic experience of thirty-three years ago. I was waiting on a bench when a young woman nurse sat down next to me, and in the most friendly way possible, started to talk with me. It was just chatter, and I'm sure that another new patient would have found it alleviated anxiety. But not me. I kept wondering why she was so friendly. Didn't she know how sick, maybe even dangerous, I was? I wanted her to go away, disappear. Or at least keep her distance, talk to someone else who wasn't so frightened, so nervous, so fearful that the dread disease could be recognized on sight. When she kept on, as warm and friendly as ever, I hoped that she would suddenly die on the spot. That would shut her up. After that I would get up and sit on another bench. Then no one could blame me for her death.

My name was called and I was led into the office of Dr. Someone or other. He was a skinny psychiatrist with a Fu Manchu moustache, and sat with both legs tucked underneath him on his well-padded chair. He asked me a series of questions, but never looked at me or changed the expression on his face. I knew I was weird, but I wasn't so young as to believe he was normal. The interview was over in just a few minutes. I was then led to another room and introduced to another doctor. He sat behind a huge desk (at least it seemed huge to me at the time), wore a white, short-sleeved shirt and smoked a cigar. He smoked a cigar just the way an uncle of mine smoked one — that is, with more interest in looking at the cigar and blowing the smoke than in the world around him.

Also in the room, tucked away in a far corner, were two other men with serious expressions on their faces, pads and pencils in hand. Who the hell were they? No one told me I was going to be treated by a group. Since they wore jackets I assumed they were inferior in status to Dr. Cigar Smoker. I attended to him.

In between puffs or those moments when Dr. Cigar Smoker fingered that cylindrical object with unusual tenderness, he asked me a series of questions. I thought it odd that none of them had any relationship to the things on my mind. The strangest of all was when he asked me to tell him what various proverbs meant. Proverbs? What the hell did that have to do with the fact that I was queer? Today I know what he was doing. He was giving me a mental status exam to see if I was psychotic or brain-damaged. Talking with me for a few minutes would have been a better idea, but I guess he was showing his students in the corner the right way to conduct an initial interview. It was sad that not one of the four doctors I met that day ever tried to show some recognition that the sixteen-year-old boy in front of them was scared out of his mind. Later, I regretted my shoddy behavior toward the friendly nurse.

I fled that place! Not until many years later did I get up the courage again to seek professional help.

How I wish this book were available to me that day. What wonderful things I would have learned. A grown-up person, someone who writes books and is called DOCTOR is telling me that I'm not such a bad person because I'm queer. (It would have been the first time I'd ever heard such a heresy.) She also tells me that I have a right to my feelings about myself and about therapy and my therapist. She tells me to trust myself and that I'm the guy who's hiring the therapist; he or she is working for me. I'm not there to please the therapist. She tells me it's OK to be scared — she tells me it's OK to feel all the things that humans feel when they seek help, when they need compassion from another human being.

You, the reader, have this book to guide you. It contains, in simple and direct language, all of the issues that are important in choosing a therapist and evaluating therapy. No one book can answer every question, but this one answers more of them than any other book I've read.

One of the strongest points in it is Hall's caution that the homophobia you feel in the therapy room may be your own, not the therapist's. Let's put the therapist aside for the moment. How can any of us grow up in society without at least *some* negative feelings about being gay? Gay Liberation helps, but doesn't always solve this leftover baggage from our early years. It's my experience in working with gay people that self-hatred comes up during various periods in a person's life, and at each resolution a more mature stage is reached.

Of course a therapist can be, and frequently is, homophobic. First of all, there is the obvious unfriendly therapist who believes that homosexuality is a signal of the deepest possible pathology. Anyone who sees such a therapist deserves what he or she gets, which will be lots of punishment and depression. But there is a new breed of therapist lurking — it's the "candy-assed" liberal who's always willing to come to the defense of gay people — just as long as gays act exactly like straights. "Mind your manners" is their unspoken message. Their condescension is not always immediately obvious since they're smart enough to know what answers to give to your questions. But the truth comes out eventually, and that's the time to leave.

I don't happen to believe that gay people have to see a gay therapist (neither does Hall). Seeing a gay therapist is very important, I believe, when the person has deep feelings of sadness of his/her gayness. But many gay people seek help for the mundane problems of living, and feel quite comfortable about their homosexuality. Any good therapist should do.

My suggestion is to read this book now, again after you choose a therapist, and again every once in a while during the course of your therapy. Reading it once won't be enough.

——I——
History
and Overview

1

Who Goes to Psychotherapy?

Lisa needed help. Her lover had left her. She'd lost her job. Her family didn't know she was gay and she had no one else to turn to. She opened up the Yellow Pages to "Psychologists," and found three pages of listings — none providing any more information than the therapist's name and address. Lisa called the first woman on the list and made an appointment, desperately hoping that the therapist would be sympathetic and non-homophobic.

If Lisa's arm had been broken, her response would have been automatic. She would have gone to a physician. If she needed legal advice, she would have contacted an attorney. Calling the therapist was a different matter. She wasn't at all certain she was doing the right thing.

In contrast to medical or legal problems, there is no standard or "correct" reason for seeking therapy. In fact, there are as many reasons for seeking therapy as there are therapy seekers. Some people contact counselors because they are depressed. Others, like Lisa, have hit snags in relationships or at work and seek support during particularly trying times. Still others are struggling to change a particular behavior — being afraid to leave the house, for example, or the compulsive use of drugs or alcohol. Or they are referred because of physical problems for which no organic basis can be found. Some come involuntarily — because they have endangered themselves or others, or because their behavior is illegal or socially repugnant. And there are those who come simply because they want a clearer understanding of what makes them tick.

Lesbians and gay men come to therapy for reasons as diverse as those mentioned above. In addition, we come because we live in a homophobic culture that contributes another layer of pain and self-doubt to the problems in living which people seek therapy to resolve.

Lesbians, Gay Men, and Psychotherapy

Gay Pride is not the revolutionary idea it was ten or fifteen years ago. Lesbians and gay men have won many victories. In urban areas particularly, we have higher expectations of acceptance from our neighbors and co-workers. Many of us have stepped out of the shadows. Hollywood has discovered us. We've been portrayed, if not ecstatically, at least sympathetically, in full-length films. Locally and nationally, our economic and political clout is something to be reckoned with. Within professional organizations of doctors, lawyers, teachers, psychotherapists and others, there are caucuses campaigning (often successfully) against homophobic policies

Apparently we can afford to be, if not complacent, at

least pleased with our progress. However, we've faced setbacks just as plentiful as our successes. Public reaction to AIDS has provided living proof that homophobia is alive and well. In contrast to the rapid mobilization for Legionnaire's Disease, which affected a tiny number of Caucasian heterosexual men, federal and state governments were painfully slow to allocate money for AIDS research. The quality of care accorded AIDS patients by some social service agencies and health care systems has been notably substandard.

Anti-gay bias is further shown in the form of continuing rejection by our families; housing and custody problems; lost jobs; and other civil rights violations. The experience of homophobia is not limited to a few gays. Over half of the 5,000 lesbians and gay men polled in a 1977 survey reported some form of harassment related to their sexual identity.

These external manifestations of homophobia are indeed dire. But perhaps even more insidious for lesbians and gays is the *internalization* of anti-gay attitudes — which results in depression, hopelessness and self-hatred. The disproportionate number of lesbians and gay men with mental health problems underscores the danger of internalized homophobia:

• In contrast with their heterosexual counterparts, gay men report more loneliness, worry, depression and less self-acceptance.

• Twenty-four percent of black homosexual men surveyed had seriously considered or attempted suicide, in contrast to two percent of black heterosexual men. White lesbians and gays consider suicide twice as often as do heterosexuals.

• Approximately thirty percent of both lesbians and gay men have alcoholism problems, as compared to twenty percent of heterosexual men and five percent of heterosexual women.

• Almost twice as many gay people go to psychotherapists as do heterosexuals.

The high percentage of lesbians and gay men who seek psychotherapy are responding predictably to the hostile conditions they face. Unfortunately, the "help" we get often adds to the problem.

Homophobia and Psychotherapy

During her first visit, the therapist Lisa had found in the Yellow Pages advised her to have sex with a man so she could "straighten out and live a normal life." Lisa left the office feeling more depressed and isolated than ever.

Fifteen years after Stonewall, homophobia continues to flourish in the offices of many therapists. This bias stems partly from Judaeo-Christian superstition, which found a comfortable niche in early psychiatric theory. It's an easy leap from sin and damnation to theories of arrested development, immaturity and pathology — the common interpretations of homosexuality by Freud and his followers.

Early psychiatrists considered us not damned, but sick. In *A General Introduction to Psychoanalysis*, Freud wrote, ". . . perverted sexuality is nothing else but infantile sexuality. . ." And Carl Jung, one of the first major theorists to diverge from Freud, added his vote to the psychiatric consensus of the day. He wrote in the early twenties, "The more homosexual a man is, the more prone he is to disloyalty and to the seduction of boys."

Many aspects of early psychiatric theory have now been deemed obsolete and abandoned. Even though anti-gay attitudes deserve to be discarded with these outmoded theories, they continue to be rescued and restored to vigor by more contemporary innovators. Eric Berne is the founder of Transactional Analysis, (T.A.) an in-the-present problem-solving approach. In *What Do You Say After You Say Hello?* (1972), Berne states that "homosexuals" frequently seek psychotherapy in order to learn "how to live more comfortably while bashing (their heads) against a stone wall."

Berne is a long way from Freud and Jung. T.A. includes no theory which labels homosexuality as pathological; presumably, its practitioners should be neutral on the subject. Berne's depiction of a gay lifestyle, however, is far from neutral. The same is equally true of the standards formulated by professional psychotherapy organizations which guide all practitioners, regardless of their theoretical orientations.

Only after the waging of an intense campaign in 1973 by gay clinicians and activists was "homosexuality" removed from the category of mental illness in the *Diagnostic and Statistical Manual of Mental Disorders* (the psychotherapist's standard reference manual published by the American Psychiatric Association). Dissatisfied with the deletion, the A.P.A. quickly substituted a modified diagnostic category: "Ego Dystonic Homosexuality." "Ego Dystonic" is psychological jargon for "it doesn't feel comfortable." Though homosexuality, *per se,* no longer ranked as a mental disorder, the majority of clinicians in the American Psychiatric Association thought that someone not comfortable with her or his homosexuality still deserved the "mental disorder" classification. Notably but predictably, there is no such category as "Ego Dystonic Heterosexuality" in the manual.

How can one account for attitudes which remain constant despite the profound transformations in the theory and practice of psychotherapy over the years?

The majority of Americans surveyed in a 1982 Gallup Poll found a gay lifestyle socially unacceptable. Negative attitudes about gay people are part of the American culture and therapists, despite their claims of an impartial, self-aware vantage point, are not culture-free. As a rule, their training merely reinforces the prejudices of a dominant culture.

In "Times Are A'Changin'," an article that appeared in *For Men Against Sexism* (1977), Claude Steiner describes his training as a psychologist: "Professionally trained therapists are prone to have extremely distorted views about homosexuality because we have been taught that it lurks at the core of emotional disturbances such as schizophrenia and alcoholism. For instance, any time that a person exhibits paranoid symptoms, I was taught to look for 'latent homosexual impulses'. . ."

A recent survey of introductory psychology textbooks substantiates Steiner's claim. Material on gay men and lesbians characteristically comes under headings that imply sickness — "sexual deviations," or "sexual dysfunctions." For every source of accurate information on lesbians and gay men, this textbook survey turned up four sources of misleading information or heterosexual bias. Only 14 of 48 introductory textbooks mentioned lesbians at all.

Polls conducted in the early 1970s indicated that most therapists approved of techniques designed to change gay sexual orientation to straight. More recently, the majority of therapists polled said they wouldn't use such techniques. This looks promising, as though some real change has occurred. But several experiments in the last few years seem to show that therapists' attitudes toward gays may not have changed — but merely gone underground.

In one such experiment, two groups of therapists were matched for age, education, experience, and treatment approach. The first group was given a set of hypothetical cases and asked to rate the subjects for severity of problems, likelihood of recovery, etc. One of the hypothetical cases included for the first group was labeled as gay.

The second group got exactly the same cases — except that the one subject labeled gay was *not* labeled gay in the second group. The first group invariably rated the "gay" person as more severely disturbed, and as having less chance of recovery, than the other group rated the same case labeled "non-gay." The results are the same when the experiment is repeated with other groups of therapists. In other words, if therapists are informed that someone is gay, they tend to believe greater mental disturbance is present.

Most therapists' attitudes toward gay people are still not gay-affirming. But the gay liberation movement has had *some* effect: Therapists now know that a new perspective on the issue exists, and that views which equate same-sex preferences with pathology are, by this new standard, "incorrect." As a result, therapists are less likely to admit that they hold such homophobic attitudes. Harder to detect, such a bias may be more insidious.

Mental health practitioners, whose identity may depend on projecting an image of themselves as tolerant and open-minded professionals, may not even be aware of their homophobia. Claude Steiner writes in "Times Are A'Changin'," that "my views were theoretically positive and emotionally negative. I believed that people have a right to choose their sexual preferences. I would never claim that homosexuality was wrong or immoral, and I felt that laws against homosexuality were wrong. But I also did not believe that homosexuals had as good a chance to be as happy as heterosexuals."

Today, if they are willing to answer direct questions about their experience and attitudes, most therapists will disclaim any bias against gay men and lesbians. But the feelings Dr. Steiner describes may not be far from the surface, and such sentiments may find subtle expression during therapy — a slight tension when a client describes a gay activity, a more relaxed attitude around non-gay subjects.

Gay men and lesbians live within a dominant culture that is homophobic and predominantly hostile. It is this atmosphere that is often the source of our stress — the reason we feel we need help. Consequently, it is essential that the help we get *does not compound our stress.* To truly help us, therapy must affirm our life choices of who we are.

There is an abundance of evidence that we've been treated abominably by the mental health profession since its inception. There is also evidence that there is now a community of therapists who will understand and respect us, who will help us to hear and honor our own inner rhythms.

Lesbian/Gay Affirmative Therapy

Over the last decade, a number of therapists have become more aware of heterosexual bias and its damaging effect on lesbian and gay clients. Many of these therapists are lesbian and gay, and have themselves been clients of heterosexually biased therapists. Their approach, called "Lesbian/Gay Affirmative Psychotherapy," is based on the belief that the choice of a lesbian or gay identity is positive, normal and healthy. This affirmation underpins and shapes every exchange within the therapy relationship. Gary's story illustrates the results of Lesbian/Gay Affirmative Therapy:

"I was nineteen and attending a small-town state university. I had no close friends to talk to about coming out and though I knew it was the right time to do it, I was scared. I went to see the campus psychologist. I was dying to come out to him and yet I found it so easy to spend every session talking about Sartre and Freud. Finally I decided that if we didn't talk about my coming out then I was going to quit therapy. At the next session, the doctor asked me, 'Are you gay?' After an eternal silence, I nodded. 'Yes, I *am* gay.'

"The doctor's initial response floored me. 'I'm here to help you find whatever it takes to make you happy,' he said immediately. 'What are the issues you want to work on?'

"I managed to stammer something about my problems in coming out, and we had a productive discussion about how to make the process easier.

"I left that session with a feeling of great accomplishment. I started on a course I have followed since."

The norms and values of the dominant culture are frequently at odds with those of lesbian and gay clients. Particularly characteristic of lesbian/gay affirmative therapists is their willingness to challenge the self-assessments of clients which are *not* based on personally relevant value systems. A lesbian went to therapy when her four-year relationship broke up, because she felt she had failed. The therapist asked her whose standards she was using to gauge "failure." She realized that she was using her parents' thirty-five year marriage as a measuring stick. She also realized that her parents were very unhappy, but had stayed together because of their children. Those values, the therapist pointed out, were not relevant to her life. Viewed in her own context, dissolving a relationship which no longer worked for either partner was a "success" — a sensible decision.

Self-Affirmative Therapy

It would be simple if all therapy failures could be laid at the collective doorstep of homophobic therapists, and all the successes attributed to lesbian/gay affirmative therapists. However, the reality is more complex. Some clients, though they sense their therapists may not feel particularly positive about their gayness, report that therapy has nevertheless been effective. And other clients claim that an active lesbian/gay affirmative approach would definitely not have been helpful.

Jack emerged from four years of psychoanalysis feeling positive about himself, his gay identity and his life choices. Yet he hadn't the foggiest idea how his therapist felt about gayness. Judging by the deafening and interminable quiet spells which had punctuated his sessions, the only thing he could be sure his therapist affirmed was silence.

For some people, self-affirmation will mean lesbian/gay affirmation; for others, it may not. And still others may feel that attitudes toward gayness have little bearing on the benefits they get from therapy.

Whether or not gay consumers want a lesbian/gay affirmative therapist, it is important to know that we now have a choice in the matter. Therapists are available to us who are keenly aware of the damage to self-esteem that results from membership in a stigmatized minority, and whose therapeutic approach incorporates such awareness. It is the first time since the inception of psychotherapy that we have had such a choice.

2

Treating Lesbians and Gay Men:
Past and Present

The Elusive Cure

It is useful to examine the kind of psychiatric and psychological treatment that lesbians and gay men have historically received, for two reasons. First, it gives consumers a tour of the shadow side of the medical-psychiatric establishment — a side invisible to most psychotherapy consumers. Such a retrospective view reveals the therapist in the role of social controller. Mavericks of any sort who cross the boundaries of convention have always run the risk of being "treated" by these guardians of the status quo.

For lesbians and gay men, such psychologically respectable "treatments" included castration and hysterectomy at the turn of the century, and lobotomy, sedation and electric shock in subsequent decades. More recently, behavioral techniques have been the treatment of choice for most psychotherapists attempting to "cure" gay

27

people. Behavioral therapists may use aversive stimuli —
a form of therapy in which the gay male client is presented
simultaneously with sexually arousing images of men and
nauseating smells, small shocks or repugnant images.
Presumably these noxious or painful stimuli, now linked
in the client's mind with his preferred sexual partners,
will break or contaminate his positive associations with
men.

Sometimes these therapies caused lesbians and gay
men to make some initial shift away from homosexual
choices. Follow-up data indicate, however, that such
changes are rarely permanent. On the subject of "cures,"
C.A. Tripp writes in *The Homosexual Matrix*, "Over the
years there have been literally dozens of second party
accounts of 'cured' homosexuality. Like the footprints of
the Loch Ness monster, they very often appear, but without the presence of the elusive beast."

As well as providing a chronicle of anti-gay attitudes,
these "cure" attempts give consumers valuable information about both the limits of psychotherapy, and the un-
willingness of many psychotherapists to admit their lack
of proficiency in areas where they clearly have none. We
can be grateful that they have failed so thoroughly in their
attempts to change sexual orientation. However, the ina-
bility of this professional group to learn from its mistakes
and acknowledge its limits raises questions about its
claims of competency in other areas. Such a clear demon-
stration of both homophobic attitudes and unresponsive-
ness to change signals should reinforce the consumer's
commitment to continuing evaluation of the therapy
experience.

The stories that follow span the last seventy years. They show that although contemporary treatment of gays does not include the mutilating "cures" of the past, the old attitudes are still evident. If the style has changed in half a century, the substance often has not.

The first story, Edward's, gives a new, somewhat macabre edge to the quip: "The surgery was successful, but the patient died." Adding to the tragedy is the fact that Edward himself, as do many lesbians and gay men, requested his "cure."

Boston: 1914: Edward loved men. Frequently his passion displaced his common sense and he would actively pursue them, gaze into their eyes, and occasionally embrace them impulsively. Because one such outburst occurred at work, he found himself, despite his skill as a professional bookkeeper, losing his job.

Believing himself to be evil and unnatural, Edward sought help from a physician. The doctor began treatment with dietary injunctions and prescribed a heavy daily dose of laxatives. The regiment also included electric shock treatments applied along his spine to his genitals.

Edward found the treatments ineffective and requested a more radical intervention. The doctor agreed and Edward's dorsal penis nerve was surgically excised. After the surgery, Edward continued to have strong erotic feelings toward men. Because of the severity and intensity of these erotic feelings, the doctor recommended that another operation be performed, this time to remove Edward's testes. After the second surgery, Edward reported no more erotic inclinations. Although he was relieved to be free at last of his obsession, he felt quite lonely. He asked the doctor to introduce him to a lady who had been surgically treated the same way for the same affliction.

Half a Century Later

Boston, 1964: Paul worked for a big advertising agency as a copywriter. He was deep in the closet at work, but active in the local bar scene. His social circle was exclusively gay. The discrepancy between his professional and his private life was so great that he became depressed and decided to get some psychiatric help. He was directed to a Freudian analyst, Dr. C., by a woman therapist he had been seeing. Dr. C. told him he would have to come every weekday for a 50 minute session, and would have to start dating women — or at the very least, terminate his sexual encounters with men.

Paul adhered to this schedule for the first year, with only occasional lapses. When it seemed to him that he wasn't getting anywhere — his dreams, his longings, his lusts were still directed toward men — Dr. C. would assure him that it was all a matter of locating his buried heterosexual impulses. These, he was told, had been repressed due to some childhood trauma which had turned him away from women. If he continued to lie on the couch, free associate and control his unhealthy impulses toward men, and began dating women, then his natural and long-buried heterosexuality would emerge.

Paul spent almost seven years on Dr. C.'s couch. During that time he discovered a great many childhood traumas. He discovered that his father had been cruel to

him, that his older sister had tormented him and that his
mother had, during a temporary separation from his
father, given the appearance of abandoning him. He
dredged up these events and all the pain associated with
them. On many days he lay on the couch and wept for the
whole session. After such occasions he would leave feeling cleansed and whole and full of new insights. He
waited eagerly for his homosexual impulses to disappear,
along with his old sense of hurt and bitterness. He was
certainly making progress, growing up, learning to accept
himself — but, strangely, he felt exactly as before toward
men. Dr. C. assured Paul that there was some other
buried memory which hadn't been reached yet. The day
would soon come. . . .

In all, Paul spent about $45,000 on psychoanalysis.
Since it lasted so long, it felt very comfortable — as much
a part of his life as his job or his apartment.

Toward the middle of the seventh year, however — by
then he was down to three times a week instead of five —
Paul met a man his own age and fell in love. Whenever he
had shown signs of becoming emotionally involved with a
male before this, Dr. C. had been able to mobilize Paul's
guilt, and nip the affair in the bud. Hearing about the
impending liaison, Dr. C. asked him, as usual, "What
does your conscience tell you about this new
relationship?"

And then, for the second or third time in seven years,
Paul became very angry. He realized he had been manipu-
lated and abused by the homophobia of the culture, which
was reflected in Dr. C. He got up from the couch, turned
to Dr. C. and said, "My conscience tells me I should walk

out of here and never come back."

He did just that — returning only once, for a brief session to explain that he was finished with analysis.

Looking back over the experience years later, Paul saw that he had been profoundly unlucky in the choice of his therapist. Where another, more enlightened analyst might have helped him come to terms with his potentially satisfying nature, Dr. C. had reinforced Paul's own worst doubts and fears. Paul had been kept in a state of mental subjection for the majority of a decade.

Lesbians have fared no better than gay men in the hands of psychotherapists. We are invalidated because of our sexuality; as women, we face the entrenched misogyny of the traditionally male psychiatric establishment. These attitudes came to light in a classic study, conducted by Inge Broverman and her colleagues in 1970.

In the study, a group of clinicians was instructed to come up with three separate descriptions: a description of a mature, healthy, socially competent woman; a description of a mature, healthy male; and a description of a third person whose gender was not specificed. The clinicians were simply to list the qualities of a mature healthy *person*. When the data were tabulated, it emerged that the composites of the healthy male and the healthy person were almost the same. The description, however, of the healthy mature woman was almost the opposite of both. She was perceived by the clinicians as more submissive, less independent, less stable, more vain, less objective than the healthy male or the healthy person.

In other words, a healthy man is a healthy person; a woman is an unhealthy person. Lesbians, therefore, carry the stigma of double deviance. We are not "normal" because we are women, and we are not "normal" women. The following stories illustrate the kind of assault lesbians face as gays and as women.

Portland, 1918: H. began psychiatric treatment two years before women won the right to vote in America. She was 26 years old at the time and a graduate of medical school. She had excelled in her course work and was well respected as a physican. In the course of her studies she learned that her attractions to women were abnormal, so she entered psychiatric therapy.

The first course of treatment, hypnotic suggestions, proved unsuccessful. H. could not be induced into a deep trance and adamantly resisted the psychiatrist's suggestions that she assume a more characteristically female role. H. feared that by accepting the suggestions, she would find herself in the more traditional circumscribed situation of most women in her times.

H. decided that she was making no progress because she was not facing the problem squarely. Her only choice was to live as a man. It was decided that a hysterectomy would be the most advisable treatment; after it was performed, H. assumed a man's appearance and went to work as a physician in a hospital. She was very successful in her work until she was recognized by an old friend and denounced. Hounded and ridiculed by the hospital staff, she fled.

Seventy Years Later

Dayton, 1978: Mike and Natalie were married in a
synagogue outside of Dayton. Sex had been disappointing
for Natalie before marriage, and being married didn't
improve things. The newlyweds set up house in Colum-
bus where Mike was a graduate student in psychology.
Searching for an explanation for her sexual unresponsive-
ness, Natalie scoured abnormal psychology textbooks and
finally decided to see a therapist. She'd been in therapy
before with a therapist who just sat there, like a Buddha,
never saying much.

Natalie didn't want another silent treatment. She
asked Mike to find the name of a therapist who did body
work. Mike's graduate advisor recommended a well-
known bioenergetic body therapist, who worked with
body blocks and physical armoring. He practiced in Cin-
cinnati, over a hundred miles away, and Natalie, not eager
to travel so far, put off the trip. Looking for a diversion,
she decided to go back to school. Among the classes she
enrolled in was a Women's Studies seminar.

On Saturday nights, Mike and Natalie usually stayed
home and invited another couple over. One Saturday their
friends Ann and Jerry passed around a joint and then Jerry
proposed an orgy. With varying degrees of enthusiasm,
everyone agreed. Natalie thought she had nothing to lose.
The encounter was more awkward than erotic, but when
Ann kissed Natalie it was an intensely exciting, mem-
orable moment. The next day, Natalie called the therapist
and made an appointment.

He was a portly, bearded man who asked Natalie to

undress and questioned her while she sat naked. She was afraid to mention what had happened with Ann. She talked exclusively about her sexual problems with her husband. When she left, she felt worse because she had not been honest.

When she went back the next time, Natalie told the therapist she had been sexually aroused by a woman. The therapist was very forceful. He told her she was definitely not a lesbian. He explained that lesbianism was a defense against men. Her sexual feelings toward Ann were, he said, simply a way of acting out some angry impulses toward her father. He then asked her to undress and reach out to him. He told her to call out her father's name. When the session was over, he hugged her and told her again that she wasn't a lesbian.

Although Natalie did not bring up her feelings with Ann, she had an increasingly difficult time avoiding the issue in her Women's Studies class. The teacher, and several of the students were lesbians and the lesbian writers on the syllabus were frequently the focus of class discussions. Looking back months later, Natalie realized she had been in the process of coming out. Ironically enough it was the therapist's emphatic denial of her feelings which made her question, and ultimately free, those feelings.

In retrospect, the encounter with the therapist seemed pivotal. It was the first time Natalie had asserted the validity of her own truth. She lost sight of it now and then during the next few years, but it has always come back again — the truth of her own body.

Treatment in the Eighties

Today, although castrations and lobotomies are no longer the reflexive treatment for homosexuality, lesbians and gay men, simply by virtue of their sexual orientation, still risk some form of homophobic response from psychotherapists. But in the last fifteen years, therapy has begun to reflect the changes in consciousness precipitated by the civil rights movement, feminism and gay liberation.

Radical Therapy was the first new therapy movement incubated in this period of social ferment. It maintained that the mental disorders of individuals were simply symptoms of a much larger social disorder. By perpetuating class, race and gender biases, and values which stressed personal achievement at the expense of cooperation, the mental health establishment compounded the disorders of society. In short, traditional therapists were the soft police who helped enforce the status quo. Social analysis is at the heart of Radical Therapy. One of its first journals rallied readers with the banner headline: Change not adjustment.

An outgrowth of the consciousness-raising groups of the early seventies was Feminist Therapy, which shares the society-as-patient perspective of Radical Therapy. It places special emphasis on the damaging effect of gender-bound roles.

The influence of both Radical and Feminist Therapies is clearly visible in Lesbian/Gay Affirmative Therapy, and even among practitioners who would not identify themselves as Radical, or Feminist, or Lesbian/Gay Affirmative. The result of this influence is a variety of genuine alternatives to traditional therapies. Some psychotherapy clients seek out such nontraditional forms of therapy. Others are fortunate enough to end up, quite inadvertently, with such therapists. The following story offers a glimpse of this new kind of therapist, along with some hope that such nontraditional approaches will become less remarkable in the future because they will be less rare.

Minneapolis, 1983: Andy had had two sexual encounters with men. The first was with his best high school friend. They had both gotten stoned in Andy's father's van, but not stoned enough to forget, afterward, what had happened. The next incident occurred during a shore leave in West Germany while Andy was in the Navy. He had never seen the man before they left the bar together that night. He never saw him again.

Before they had gotten engaged, Andy told Denise about both episodes. Unperturbed, she responded by quoting Kinsey statistics about the universality of such experiences. Her confidence began to wane when their engagement lengthened into years and Andy continued to postpone the wedding date. His parents, too, were tired of waiting. Older, now, they wanted a grandchild. Andy felt their urgency. He was thirty-one.

In the deepest recesses of his mind, Andy knew he preferred men. How else could he explain the recurring memories of his two encounters, which, compared to the prosaic sex with Denise, had electrified and stunned him? Andy found that accepting his preference was another matter altogether. He decided to go to a counselor —

someone who could provide the magic pill that would make him shape up, make him "normal."

In Ben's office, Andy began a breathless recital of his childhood memories. If he could remember all the details, perhaps they could discover the "source" of the problem, root it out, fix it; whatever it was that shrinks did.

Gently, Ben responded that he would like to review Andy's past. . . not because it held the clue to his preference for men but because it might explain *why* he felt the way he did *about* his attractions.

It was a subtle difference in phrasing and emphasis, but it had a powerful effect. Was Ben suggesting, Andy wondered, that there was more than one way to feel about his sexuality?

After Andy had talked about his family's solid Midwestern belief in God and country, and their expectation that he, their only son, would marry and perpetuate the family name, Ben commented that there probably was no latitude in such a family, or in the community in which Andy was raised, for any alternative values.

When Andy talked about sex with Denise, Ben acknowledged that the experience sounded warm, if not galvanic. Then he asked about the experiences Andy had had with men. At first, Andy responded with one-liners: "We smoked dope and did it" and "I met him in a bar and we went to his apartment."

Ben didn't accept these abbreviated versions. He interrogated Andy: What had attracted him in the first place? Had they talked about the attraction? Who proposed sex? What exactly had they done sexually? How had the caresses felt? The kisses? His orgasm? What had happened afterward?

As he disclosed these details, Andy realized that the encounters had felt so shameful that he had numbed himself to much of his actual experience. By encouraging a recounting of the details, Ben conveyed his conviction that the encounters were valid, deserving of attention and appreciation.

Ben did not do anything dramatic. In a consistent, thoughtful way he presented another framework for viewing the same events and feelings Andy had regarded unhappily as constraints which would keep him forever from the promised land of family approval and "normality." Gradually, Andy began to accept his attraction to men.

Telling Denise that he wanted to explore his gay feelings was the hardest thing Andy had ever done. It was only the beginning of a painful change process.

The first time Andy went to a gay dance, he met Jim. They spent an intensely happy week together. Then Jim's lover, who had been on a business trip, returned; as suddenly as he had materialized in Andy's life, Jim disappeared.

After several more disappointments, Andy joined a men's group. In addition to Ben's counsel, he found he needed peer support to confront some of the harsh realities he was encountering. It wasn't easy to find somebody steady; he missed the intimacy he had had with Denise; he was terrified, as was everyone else he met, of AIDS.

Though these issues still troubled Andy when he

stopped seeing Ben, the concern which had brought him to therapy was resolved. Andy accepted himself as a gay man.

Andy was lucky. By chance, he ended up with a counselor who was both skilled and gay affirmative. Luck may always play a role in finding a good therapist, but there are ways that we, as consumers, can limit our dependency on chance. The following chapter outlines some ways for us to avoid the kind of homophobic therapy experiences many of us, as lesbian and gay consumers, have encountered.

3

The Therapy Marketplace:
Philosophies and Methods of Treatment

The psychotherapy scene today is a blend of magic and technology, tradition and innovation. An exotic bazaar, it features a staggering assortment of therapy styles, philosophies and techniques — and *choices for the consumer.* Faced with the task of choosing from this array, most therapy seekers use whatever guide is handiest. Some question friends who have been through therapy. Those in urban areas check gay directories or bulletin boards. People without access to such referral sources must rely on more general sources: local medical associations, clinics, or even the Yellow Pages.

The therapy seeker looking for a compatible therapist with a compatible approach faces an obstacle course: how to decide which type of counselor will be most helpful? How to find a nearby counselor who provides such treatment for affordable fees? What *is* the best therapy method, anyway? Even those who practice it disagree.

41

Some psychotherapists believe that therapy is about changing behavior that is visible and measurable. Some see therapy as a magical encounter, an existential wrestling match through which both therapist and client emerge more fully human. Other counselors consider themselves social analysts, who place their clients' issues in the context of the social and cultural forces that have shaped them. Still other psychotherapists believe that their patients' problems are "mental disorders" which can be cured by nothing less than a major personality overhaul. The majority of therapists mix several techniques, blending science, art, skill, intuition, vision.

The diversity of style and approach that characterizes all of psychotherapy is no less true of counselors who work with lesbian/gay clientele.

The New Eclecticism

A survey of therapists taken twenty years ago would have turned up clear definitions, staunch allegiances, and well-defined territories. Some would have labeled themselves psychoanalysts, others behaviorists, others Gestalt therapists or Jungians. Today, most therapists label themselves "eclectic." They blend. They borrow. They are not purists. Every therapist has a different repertoire of techniques to be used in unique combinations. Techniques vary. One therapist explores her client's dreams; another directs his client's attention to an empty chair, suggesting dialogue with an imaginary parent; another focuses her client's attention on his breathing.

Therapy techniques also involve time frames. Some therapists believe that change should occur within the

space of a few sessions; others think any therapy that lasts
less than a few years is necessarily superficial and can't
lead to lasting change.

Change has to do, too, with the client-therapist con-
figuration. Some practitioners maintain that change can
occur when there is one therapist and one client. Others
insist there is no change possible which doesn't include a
social network — a family or a group — in treatment.
Every change formula has its advocates. Most represent a
blend of several styles and philosophies.

However eclectic the technique, the type of treatment a therapist offers is shaped by his or her basic perspective about what causes change. There is no simple
way to categorize these perspectives, but there are three
orientations that best represent the marketplace.

The first orientation is based on the belief that
feelings — uncovering and expressing them — is the key
to change.

A second perspective emphasizes new *behavior* as the
source of change. The techniques of this orientation
involve the development of new behavioral skills and
patterns.

The third perspective emphasizes *thinking*. According to proponents of this orientation, change occurs as
new maps of reality are drawn, correcting the distorted
world view previously held by the client.

Though these three orientations — *feeling, thinking*
and *behaving* — require very different approaches to therapy, ultimately they lead to the same place. If change
starts in one arena, most therapists agree it will spill over
into another and then another. If we think about our-

selves differently, we can't fail to feel differently and then behave differently. If we start by changing our behavior, we'll begin to feel and think differently about ourselves and the world.

The cross-pollination among orientations in the last two decades makes it unlikely that a therapist who emphasizes one approach would disclaim the usefulness of a different one. And generally eclectic therapists will adjust the approach they use to the needs of the client.

An especially controversial approach involves the use of drugs for therapy. This method is discussed at the end of this chapter.

The Feeling Cure

Jane grew up in a family of alcoholics. When she was fifteen, she ran away and got married. The marriage broke up a couple of years later and Jane got a job assembling circuit boards in an electronics factory, supporting herself for the first time. When she was twenty-one, a new union representative — who did not go out of her way to hide the fact that she was a dyke — began processing grievances in Jane's unit. Jane liked this woman, Rio, and began to do some volunteer work for the union. After several months of working together on a membership drive, they went home together. Six weeks later they were living together.

Jane's relationship with Rio was different from anything in the past. Rio was attentive and supportive. Jane was happier than she'd ever been. Around the time of their first anniversary, Rio began encouraging Jane to transfer to the Quality Assurance section of the company they worked for, so Jane would have more opportunity for advancement. Alternately, Rio urged her to get into a union office and do work like Rio's.

Jane, who'd never graduated from high school, decided that the first step was to get her General Equivalency Diploma. As soon as Jane began going to night school things grew tense between her and Rio. Rio was used to eating dinner with Jane, and complained about Jane's being off at school in the evenings. When Jane got her diploma and started junior college, Rio accused her of not caring about her. The relationship started falling apart.

The instructor of one of the psychology courses Jane was taking conducted the class like a therapy group. Jane said little during the class, but listening to her classmates talk about relationship patterns made her wonder about her own. When her fights with Rio became violent, Jane made an appointment to see her instructor alone. He recommended counseling, and suggested an older woman who worked in the college counseling center.

Jane liked Margot immediately. She reminded Jane of a grade school teacher who'd given Jane lots of special attention. She fantasized that Margot would do the things she'd wanted her teacher to do — make a fuss over her, dress her in the morning, hug her and tuck her in at night.

After a few sessions, Jane's fantasies collided violently with reality. She was only getting forty-five minutes a week — and that was because it was Margot's job. Jane's initial feelings of warmth towards Margot evolved into a conviction that Margot didn't care about her, that she was only one in a parade of clients. Jane refused to talk for several sessions. Margot said she could understand how

Jane was feeling, that the pain of years couldn't be easily undone.

During the next few months, Jane was angry; Margot was consistently supportive and warm. Then one day Jane began to cry in the throes of an especially painful memory. Margot put her arm around her. That small gesture broke down Jane's wall of mistrust; after that, when she cried in sessions, Margot usually held her. For the next year and a half, the counselor's office was a place where Jane's feelings, no matter how unpredictable or intense, were all that mattered.

Jane's therapist worked primarily with feelings. She considered empathy — the understanding, acceptance and reflection of clients' feelings — to be the critical element in therapy. According to this approach, healing and growth are built into the human organism, and like well-nourished plants, people who are treated lovingly will grow into their potential.

Many therapists who prefer a feeling focus favor active, physical ways of eliciting clients' feelings. Body therapists, for instance, believe that emotions are accessible by breathing and assuming certain physical postures; other therapists favor pillow hitting, role playing, certain hypnotic techniques, or yelling as ways of gaining access to and expressing long pent-up emotions.

Several therapy approaches share the common starting point of feelings. The differences between these approaches emerge from the methods used to elicit feelings from the client, and how the discharge of these feelings is guided and evaluated. Some therapists believe that catharsis itself is healing. For others the expression of feelings is useful only if it enhances rational understanding or leads to changed behavior.

Also dramatically different are the styles of "feeling" therapists. They can be chilly or warm, provocative or passive. The common denominator is their belief that change begins with the expression of a client's feelings.

Thinking Approaches

Tim went to see Perry, a clinical psychologist, because he was having trouble with his lover's son, an eight-year-old who stayed with them on weekends and holidays. Jamal would burst in on them early Saturday and Sunday mornings, wake them both up, and get between them in bed.

Tim hadn't been around kids before. He was furious with Jamal's behavior, but he tried to conceal it. When Tim mentioned his feelings to his lover, Curtis promised to limit Jamal's Saturday morning incursions. By the next Saturday, however, Curtis had forgotten his promise and Jamal was, again, in bed with them at dawn.

By the time Tim went to see Perry, he was ready to explode. He felt he had no options, that his life was being run by an eight-year-old.

Perry asked Tim to figure out where he'd gotten the idea that he had no rights in the situation. Tim remembered his own family, where his mother had done the disciplining and his father hadn't considered it his right to intrude on what had been defined as his wife's turf. It became evident during therapy that Tim had learned in his childhood that there was one "real" parent who took

care of children, and one nominal parent who made an appearance now and then.

Perry thought Tim's abdication of his own needs was
based on a distorted view that Tim had acquired in his
own family. Based on his own early experiences, Tim had
concluded that only Curtis had a right to engage his son,
or shape his behavior. It was important, Perry said, for
Tim to become a real person to Jamal — a person with
needs and preferences. If he didn't, his relationship with
Curtis would suffer more.

Perry suggested that Tim talk the plan over with
Curtis, and then that they make a special date to talk to
Jamal together about the new rules in the house. Tim was
delighted when Curtis agreed to the plan.

Tim and Curtis told Jamal that he was to fix his own
breakfast and to entertain himself until 9 AM on Saturday
and Sunday mornings. Tim and Curtis would get up then,
and they could all do something together. If Jamal failed to
observe the new rule, he wouldn't be allowed to ride his
bike around the neighborhood that weekend. It took two
weeks of grounding before Jamal observed the new rule.
Much to Tim's surprise, Jamal seemed more responsive to
him after that, and their relationship became closer and
more relaxed.

Perry pegged Tim's situation as a thinking problem. By
changing Tim's perspective, his behavior changed, allowing him to feel better about his lover's son.

There are several therapeutic approaches which
conclude that problems in functioning stem from errors in
thinking. By confronting clients about their perceptual

distortions, exaggerations and misapplications from the past, therapists help clients to develop a more accurate map of reality. Once the distortions are corrected, dysfunctional behavior fades.

Another source of perceptual distortion, according to some practitioners, stems from unfamiliar feelings, thoughts, or behavior, which are actually "normal," but are perceived by the client as being "abnormal." Because these sensations may be frightening, they often earn the undeserved label of "problem." The task of the therapist in such situations is, by means of redefinition, to convert the "problem" into a nonproblem. The counselor must show the client that this new way of thinking or feeling, alarming as it is, is both "normal" and, under the circumstances, predictable.

Neil entered therapy because he could not become sexually aroused. The therapist found that to Neil, this lack of arousal meant that he was inadequate — a bad partner. After taking a history, and finding that he had always performed on request in the past, the therapist gave Neil's nonarousal a new definition.

The therapist concluded that Neil's past fears of nonresponsiveness had caused him to ignore the variations in his own feelings. He had often had sex when he hadn't felt like it. Now, the therapist said, Neil's body was actually doing him a favor. It was saying no for him, allowing him the time and space to catch up with his feelings. It was, according to the therapist, a state to be encouraged rather than discouraged. The therapist told Neil to say no even more often.

The effect of prescribing the precise symptom which Neil had brought in to shed was useful. Neil no longer saw himself as inadequate; instead he was taking care of himself. His anxiety dissolved, and with it, the problem.

Cognitive approaches provide new or redefined maps of reality; maps which sometimes challenge or contradict those previously developed by clients. The names of the thinking therapies — Cognitive Therapy, Rational Emotive Therapy, Reality Therapy — provide a tip-off, a preview for consumers of coming attractions.

New ways of charting social reality are particularly important to people whose membership in certain groups — lesbians and gay men, blacks, and women — have traditionally meant devalued status. Consequently, it is difficult to imagine any version of feminist or ethnic or gay affirming therapy which does not include, at least in part, a thinking approach — a social analysis that illuminates a new social reality.

Behavioral Approach

The day after the police department, upon the advice of the local health department, had received rubber gloves and masks to deal with AIDS victims, Alan got sick while eating in a gay restaurant. When the waiter brought dessert he felt a wave of nausea which made speech impossible. His heart was thudding, his mouth went dry. He excused himself to his friends and left.

Alan went straight to bed, and told his friends later that he'd had the 24-hour flu. The next time he had a wave of nausea, it was a hot day and he was in the subway on the way home from work. Everybody was in shirtsleeves and the car was stifling. He was sandwiched between three or four passengers, one a sallow, emaciated man who looked ill.

After that Alan began to take cabs to work. He made excuses to his friends about having extra work to do, and began avoiding social encounters of any kind. He learned that crowds were likely to incapacitate him. Gradually he eliminated all activities which triggered the disabling anxiety. He felt depressed, isolated and off balance at work. His encounters with coworkers seemed stilted. He was self-conscious and afraid he would display some inappropriate emotion. He began to think he was being treated as though he were a "case."

Alan had a good relationship with his supervisor, and they talked about his feelings of panic. The supervisor agreed to grant Alan's request for a temporary leave as long as he agreed to get counseling.

Alan's behavioral therapist began by teaching him a series of relaxation exercises which were taped in the office so Alan could use them at home. Then the therapist asked Alan to catalog all the fearful situations he was experiencing and rank each one on the basis of the anxiety it caused him. Alan was instructed, during a therapy session, to start by imagining the least fearful — a trip to the local mom and pop grocery for a carton of milk. Then he was to conjure up as much anxiety as possible, duplicating, if he could, the waves of fear which might come up during such an excursion. When Alan could feel some of the fear, the therapist asked him to start using certain relaxation techniques he had practiced. Alan focused on his breathing, directing his awareness to different parts of his body, as he tensed and relaxed his muscles.

Eventually Alan was able to control his anxiety in certain situations and could resume some of his usual activities. He started going to a restaurant where he could order take-out food, and then started having coffee with a friend in whom he could confide. Gradually his circle expanded and, though his anxiety never disappeared, it no longer overwhelmed him. He chose to stay away from the most frightening situations on the list: gay bars and large parties. They remained overwhelming, and he adjusted his lifestyle to avoid them.

According to certain therapy approaches, all behavior is shaped by learning principles. That is, we are rewarded for some things and punished for others. Our own anxiety can fall into the punishment category. So if we have become anxious by behaving a certain way, we may not want to do it again. Alan was frightened first by his fear of AIDS, then by its association with gay men, then by people in general.

With very specific assignments, behavioral therapists drain the punishment from the behavior by approaching what is frightening in small steps, or by pairing it with rewards or a feeling state (relaxation) which cannot co-exist with panic.

Therapists who treat phobias or offer ways to break habits are usually behavioral therapists. Assertiveness training, or any therapy which focuses on acquisition of new skills, falls under the heading of behavioral therapy.

At the risk of oversimplification, some of the more well-known schools of therapy are shown in figure A,

DIFFERENT THERAPY APPROACHES

Lesbian/Gay Affirmative Therapy

Feminist Therapy

Feeling Therapies	*Thinking Therapies*	*Behavior Therapies*
Body Therapies	Cognitive Therapy	Aversion Therapy
Client-Centered Therapy (Rogerian)		Relaxation Therapy
Gestalt Therapy		Assertiveness Training
		Behavior Modification
Psychoanalysis	Reality Therapy	
Existential Therapy	Rational Emotive Therapy	
Jungian Analysis		
	Strategic Therapy	
Transactional Analysis		

Figure A

grouped under the perspectives of *feeling, thinking* and *behavior.* Some approaches, as you can see, cannot be limited to one perspective — in fact they may span two or more.

Chemical Therapy

The subject of drugs is controversial for several reasons. First, it concentrates the power of cure in the hands of a medical establishment, which has been even more retrograde than other mental health fields when it comes to recognition of the social causes of problems.

Second, many physicians have overprescribed with disastrous effects. Forty-three percent of adults in America today use mood changing drugs prescribed by physicians. The majority of addiction problems in the U.S. are from prescription drugs.

Such drugs fall into three categories: major tranquilizers, such as Thorazine and Stelazine, prescribed for psychoses — states in which people have dramatic breaks with day-to-day reality; minor tranquilizers like Librium and Valium, commonly prescribed for anxiety; and the antidepressants which include Elavil and Triavil.

Not uncommonly, people who use these drugs report various unpleasant side effects such as fatigue, blurriness of vision, constipation, dry mouth, and loss of coordination. Taken over the long term, major tranquilizers can result in permanent neurological damage. The minor tranquilizers can cause brain and liver damage. The long term effects of antidepressants, which are relatively new, have not yet been determined.

Balancing some of the negative consequences is the fact that for some people, the quality of life without chemical therapy is intolerable. According to the researchers who specialize in biochemistry, congenital chemical anomalies, rather than early traumas or family problems, account for the variations in individuals' coping abilities. Exponents of this psycho-physiological perspective argue that "talk" therapy doesn't address the real problem; chemical shortcomings, they insist, deserve a chemical approach.

The Chemical Approach

Stephanie had taught junior high school for fifteen years and was a captain in the Reserves. She had a diverse group of friends, most of whom she'd known since she had first come to Detroit right after college. Stephanie's parents accepted her lesbianism and made it very clear that they considered Janet, her partner of seven years, part of the family.

There was nothing Stephanie could point to, no circumstances in her life which accounted for the chronic feelings of inadequacy and hopelessness. Convinced that she had some unresolved early issue to work out, some inexpressible anger at her father for preferring her younger brother, or at her mother for being too eager to compensate for lost affection of her father, she began psychotherapy.

The therapist she chose was eclectic and tried several different approaches. First they sorted through Stephanie's early life with the help of some picture albums. She relived some of the pain of early experiences, particularly her disappointment when she was consigned to her mother's domestic world by default. She remembered the agony of high school encounters with boys who wanted more from her than the apprehension they elicited.

Stephanie felt temporarily relieved during these therapy sessions, but that relief disappeared quickly. Less than an hour after each session, the same tide of melancholy would engulf her. The therapist shifted her focus to the present. Stephanie began to report her weekly events, to keep a diary charting the rhythms of her depression to see if they correlated with anything specific in her life. No patterns emerged. The therapist recommended a masseuse who also did acupuncture. When that didn't help, the therapist began simply listening and commiserating with Stephanie.

Stephanie had a chronic sleeping problem which began to get worse. She could fall asleep easily, but would wake up early in the morning, and be unable to sleep again. Her interest in sex disappeared and she began to complain of numbness in her body.

The therapist referred Stephanie to a psychiatrist at a local clinic. After an evaluation and medical examination he prescribed an anti-depressant medication. In a few weeks, Stephanie began to feel sexual again, to sleep better, and to be interested in food. Her depression receded. She felt as though she was living in the real world for the first time in years. Though she liked her therapist, she felt the therapy process itself had been useful only because it had kept her alive during the grimmer moments; it had not affected her mood. She stopped therapy and continued to take the medication.

Drugs have long been used oppressively against gays and

women. For every positive case there are scores of women strung out on Valium because M.D.'s, plagued by vague complaints, didn't have the time to listen between the lines. Despite this misuse of drugs, many therapists, if pressed, will agree that for some people no amount of talk therapy has been successful. For some of these therapy dropouts, chemical therapy has been dramatically effective. To evaluate the usefulness of drugs, they must be liberated from their "good" and "bad" roles; they must be viewed with less passion and more perspective.

An aid to developing such a perspective is a large tome called the *Physicians Desk Reference*. Issued every year, it lists all the reported side effects of prescription drugs. If your prescribing M.D. doesn't have one available, check the library. The library may be a source of other drug data as well. If drugs are the treatment of choice, it's important to be well informed about them.

The Choice is Yours

Feeling, thinking, behavior and chemical therapies — they are commonly used therapy techniques, and understanding them will help you make your way through the therapy bazaar. Before starting, consider which approach, or combination of approaches, best seems to suit your needs. Ask your new therapist to describe her or his approach and compare it to the one you want to use.

Continue evaluating as you go. If an approach that works well for you in the beginning of therapy loses its effectiveness in later sessions, reconsider the choices. Pay attention to your needs. Ultimately, they are the compass which will guide you through the psychotherapy bazaar.

—4—
Individual, Couple and Group Therapy:
What to Expect, How to Choose

"The Doctor is in," announces Lucy, and she charges Charlie Brown a nickel for a bit of heartless advice. Charles Schultz, Woody Allen and others have brought therapy — or some version of it — into the mainstream of American culture. The couch, the framed diplomas, the bewildered patient, the officious therapist: this tableau represents therapy in most people's minds. Confronted regularly by such pop renditions, we may, as consumers, have trouble separating myth from reality. What forms does psychotherapy actually take? Which is the best choice?

One way to choose among different modes of therapy is to evalute your reasons for seeking therapy. If you want to examine personal characteristics that trouble you, individual therapy is probably a good place to start. If you see your problem in interactional terms — for example, difficulty with a lover — including your partner in couples' therapy may provide some immediate relief. Finally, if your source of problems seems to lie in a particular aspect of your identity — being gay, or lesbian, even more specifically, being a minority within a minority, e.g., a gay man of color, or a gay or lesbian teenager — a group of similarly identified people may be most useful. Of course, this is a rough guideline; unlike the different modes of therapy described in this chapter, people's problems cannot be divided so neatly into separate categories and solutions.

One-to-One Therapy: Seeing the Therapist Alone

"My real training began after I finished my psychiatric residency," a psychiatrist comments. "That was when I shed the role of doctor and started seeing people as people rather than patients. Before that I felt like I'd been trapped inside a stereotype."

The one-to-one therapist/client relationship lends itself to stereotyping because the roles of client and counselor are relatively fixed and the flow of information is decidedly one-sided. The extent to which different therapists reveal themselves to clients varies, but no matter how self-disclosing they are, odds are these therapists know more about each client than those clients will ever know about the therapist. Such a deliberate focus on the client may evoke feelings and thoughts which, in the past, had neither the audience nor the opportunity to emerge.

Some clients attribute the insights that occur in one-to-one therapy to the "hot seat" techniques of their counselors. But equally significant revelations are reported by clients whose therapists take pains to remain passive, to maintain a neutral attitude. The goal of such counselors is to provide a blank screen upon which the client can project residual feelings from other important relationships, usually involvements with parents. According to some therapists and clients, it is the evocation of these long-simmering feelings which accounts for the intensity of the one-to-one therapy process.

Whether the therapist focuses actively on the client or stays invisible, the one-to-one relationship offers a unique opportunity to explore your own feelings and experiences in an arena relatively free of social expectations. Describing the process of individual psychotherapy, author and psychotherapist Sheldon Kopp writes: "The therapist can interpret, advise, provide the emotional acceptance and support that nurtures personal growth, and above all, he can listen. I do not mean that he can simply hear the other, but that he will *listen* actively and purposefully, responding with the instrument of his trade, that is, with the personal vulnerability of his own trembling self. This listening is that which will facilitate the patient's telling of his tale, the telling that can set him free."

Marge's story illustrates the liberating effect of one-to-one therapy and the personal exploration it fosters.

On the same day that Marge's lover announced that she was accepting a year's fellowship at an out-of-state university, Marge's seventeen-year-old daughter, Kristie, said that she too intended to move out. She had already made plans to live with friends and get a job.

Suddenly facing the grim prospect of living alone in what had been a full and active household, Marge forbade Kristie to leave before she was eighteen. A week later, when Marge was at an evening meeting, Kristie moved out. Soon afterward, Marge got a terse note from her daughter telling her not to worry and that she'd write soon again. There was no return address.

Feeling shaky and depressed, Marge got the name of a feminist counselor who, she learned, also had a teenage daughter. Marge spent the first few sessions alternating between sadness and anger.

The counselor shared the anguish she'd experienced when, at thirteen, her own daughter had started wearing makeup and putting down her mother's feminist values. During the course of therapy, Marge remembered her own difficult emancipation from her family as a young woman. She was flooded with old feelings of anger at her parents and recalled her conviction at the time that her departure from home was essential. This vivid recollection of her past drained some of the anger Marge felt toward Kristie. She began to view her daughter's departure more objectively — as a necessary rite of passage.

Marge spent six months in therapy. She left it feeling that she and her counselor had journeyed together over territory that would have been far more desolate had she been a solo traveler. She was embarking on a new relationship with her daughter; even more important was the new relationship she was developing with herself.

In short: Individual therapy is most useful to clients who want a refuge, a time to explore themselves with someone who creates an atmosphere that is congenial to such investigation. Other forms of therapy deal more directly with behavior change and the social aspects of living.

The Therapist as Relationship Counselor

Despite the urging of friends tired of hearing about his domestic squabbles, one man vowed never to set foot in a couple counselor's office. He was afraid that, as bad as things were between him and his lover, close scrutiny would only make them worse. Couple therapists were, he said, usually divorce — not marriage — counselors. Everyone he knew who had gone in paired had come out single.

Indeed, such counselors may see their role as the person who helps the partners say the unsayable, to look at issues that have been too painful to acknowledge. If negative feelings have been undercover for a while, such an airing may reveal irreconcilable differences: differences that make the relationship unworkable.

Such was the case with Brad and Jorge, who had been together for eleven years. Their friends saw them as an island of stability in a sea of changing relationships. For newly-formed couples in their gay community, Brad and Jorge's relationship was a model of how wonderful a gay relationship could be. After years of struggle, Brad and Jorge had even won acceptance from both sets of parents. Recently though, the two of them had begun drifting apart — seeing other lovers, heading in new directions. Yet they were not ready to let go of the investment they'd made in each other.

The family counselor they visited focused on the feelings of personal failure felt by each as he contemplated an end to the relationship. Though everyone feels sadness in such situations, the counselor said that gays tended toward a special sense of failure. Jorge and Brad's relationship had been a defiant statement to a culture which insists that gay men are unstable and promiscuous. They had made it work without any of the social supports available to heterosexual couples.

Jorge and Brad came to see how they had become tokens — they'd been carrying the banner of respectability for a whole group of people who felt devalued. And now they were carrying a sense of failure for that same group. Airing these previously unstated burdens made it easier for Brad and Jorge to part.

As well as providing a safe place to mention the unmentionable, to look at the possibility of THE END, couples counselors may serve other functions. They can help partners to untangle the past from the present, to separate realistic expectations from those pie-in-the-sky hopes no partner can ever fulfill.

The couples counselor who has worked with gay and lesbian couples may provide a perspective unavailable in any of the heterosexual marriage manuals. Every gender combination, whether male/female, male/male or female/female, has its blind spots. Women, for example, have been socialized to be sensitive to interpersonal cues, to value relationships highly, to be nurturing and non-confrontive. When two women get together, the meshing of all these interpersonal skills may create an instant and intense rapport. Lesbian therapists are likely to know from their own experiences and those of others that there is another side to this wonderful, instant intimacy. It takes very little time for a union in which the partners have been trained to express only positive feelings — and swallow anger — to turn into a nightmare of suffocation and resentment.

Couples therapists can make safe an expression of differences, of anger. The therapy can reinforce the importance, both in and out of the session, of independence — of friends and activities pursued independently of one's partner.

Jill and Kathy met at a law school party and promptly fell in love. On the rare occasions when they socialized with others, they stayed entwined all evening. After several months, their friends were turned off by such relentless ardor, and they stopped calling. Neither woman cared.

It wasn't until Casey, Jill's ex-lover from Boston, came to stay with them that Jill and Kathy had their first row. Kathy couldn't stand Casey and couldn't understand how Jill could have chosen her for a lover or a friend. Soon after Casey left, Kathy started feeling that Jill was less sexually attracted to her. They began to argue constantly; most of their fights ended with Jill walking out of the house. When Kathy got particularly upset during one fight, Jill suggested that they move apart. Kathy took half a bottle of aspirin. At the hospital, they got the name of a couples counselor.

The counselor discussed with Jill and Kathy the effects of homophobia on lesbian relationships — the tendency it creates in lesbians to retreat from a difficult world and expect lover relationships to provide a friend, a lover, and a new and improved parent. The burnout that often ensues, she said, should not be surprising. The counselor asked Jill and Kathy to experiment by sleeping separately for a week and spending an evening apart — each seeing an old friend neglected since the relationship had started.

Jill and Kathy went to therapy for two and a half months. They still skirmished, but less frequently and less intensely; they learned how to declare a truce when the old, destructive feelings started escalating, and they took some useful time apart.

In describing the difference between individual and couples therapy, one therapist said, "With individuals, the person is my client. With couples, the client is the relationship between the two people."

Most heterosexual relationships become the business of parents and in-laws, of friends, coworkers, and sometimes employers. Gay and lesbian relationships are often invisible. If family members are aware of them, they often wish that they weren't. Gay people may not always get much support for their relationships from their friends: ex-lovers can be jealous; friends may resent the sudden unavailability of an old chum. And gay couples often feel uneasy in a social environment in which lovers can turn into friends and friends into lovers.

The couples counselor may be the only historian for gay and lesbian couples. She or he may be the only person who observes our relationships over time — the only one who can say, "Couples with issues like yours can try such and such," "I've seen this aspect of your relationship change." The therapist gives our unions some social weight, some visibility. One therapist said he thought his

primary use in couples' therapy was as a validator and ex-
officio priest. Nothing in his experience compared to the
high he and his clients felt, he said, when he could tell
them, "I think you've got something good here, something really positive."

Getting Help in Groups

In *Torch Song Trilogy*, the main character, Arnold Bec-
koff, is hesitant to become lovers with a man who is in individual therapy. "Not that I got anything against analysis,"
he says. "It's a great way to keep from boring your friends."

Arnold puts his finger on one of the reasons why, for
many people, group therapy is the preferred mode. Your
individual therapist is paid to see you positively, to listen
to the ruminations that might be boring your friends.
Some of your less endearing attributes — the qualities
that alienate those close to you — may never come to
light in the course of individual therapy. The members of
a group are less likely to bathe you in unconditional love.
If you complain a lot, you'll hear about it. If you don't say
enough, you'll probably hear about that too.

Who Goes to Groups? Lesbians and gay men, who share
both a common identification and the discrediting by
society of that identification, may crave the feelings of
validation evoked by participating in groups of peers.
Other candidates for group therapy include lesbians and
gay men who want a nonbar arena for meeting people and
developing social skills, for pursuing special interests, or
for facing problems common to particular groups such as
lesbian mothers or gay youth.

Groups may also benefit clients who need more structure than an hour once or even several times a week — for
example, people who have trouble functioning in a day-to-
day way, or who are suicidal. For such clients, individual
therapy does not provide enough support. All-day, everyday group programs, or residential treatment centers like
hospitals or halfway houses may be necessary adjuncts to
individual treatment. Addictions, too, are more
effectively treated in groups.

Group therapy may help individuals who have been
devalued and labeled "outsiders" by the dominant culture
to set their own norms, to belong, to be insiders.

"I had been in and out of therapy for depression and
social isolation for most of my life," says Marcie. "Somebody, I don't remember who, suggested that I try a
women's group. I finally heard of a woman who was
starting one and it took every ounce of guts I had to go to
that first meeting. It was very frightening; for much of
that first year I didn't speak about myself. But I was getting used to relating to people, learning to be encouraging
and nurturing of other people.

"The group was a safer place to practice than in the
outside world. I was hearing all these other womens'
stories. Their backgrounds and some of the details were
different, but the patterns were the same as mine. That
was an eye-opener. I was beginning to develop my own
feminism. I began to see connections between me and the
women in the group. Plus it was like having a safety net, a
place where I could feel little and scared. The rest of the
week I needed to feel competent and in control. I went for
five years. Since then I've been in one group or another

and they've all been extremely important to me."

A therapy group can be a place of refuge, a place to share the most private aspects of oneself, a place to practice social skills, to get support for changing behavior. People go to groups for a variety of reasons, and that provides the diversity which makes groups so productive. A gay men's group, which has been meeting in New York City for several years, reflects this diversity:

David, 31, came to therapy to find out what he really wanted from a relationship. He'd never had a sexual experience with anyone besides the lover he'd been with for seven years. He came to the group to figure out whether he was actively choosing his partner and this lifestyle, or just maintaining a safe, familiar routine.

Manuel, 27, had come out in high school. After two years of around-the-clock experimentation, he'd burned out. For the next six years, he'd stayed away from sexual relationships completely. He came to the group to explore the possibility of having relationships with men again — this time he was looking for something different from the casual sex he'd explored before.

Michael, 45, had a history of drug abuse and alcoholism. He was a member of several other groups: Narcotics Anonymous to support his continued abstinence from drugs, and a Hepatitis B support group to help him deal with chronic hepatitis as well as the recent diagnosis of chronically enlarged lymph nodes — one of the preliminary signs of AIDS. For Michael, a gay men's counseling group was part of his survival network. He needed all the support he could get to stay clean, to stay alive.

Josh, 38, was the "other man" in a triangle. A year ago,

he'd fallen in love with someone who was in a ten-year-old relationship. Randy only visited Josh when he wanted quick sex or needed a favor, yet Josh hung on. His individual therapist had said he wouldn't see Josh any more unless he started meeting new people, so Josh joined the group.

Lisle, 30, had never wanted to be gay. He had been ridiculed as effeminate and beaten up regularly while growing up. As soon as he finished college, he started looking for a therapist who would agree to help him change his sexual identity. He went through averse conditioning, a Christian reprogramming group, and even got a woman friend to go with him for sex therapy. Nothing worked. His best friend, who was straight, finally told Lisle that he'd be better off if he tried to accept who he was. For him the group was a place to review his stereotypes, to define himself in a new way.

Lesbian and Gay Group Issues. Describing her first Daughters of Bilitis lesbian meeting in 1960, one woman said, "It was a thrill because it was the first time I hadn't skulked down some dark street, been ogled by some macho mafioso on my way into a gay bar. It was the first time I didn't feel like a criminal for who I was."

For gay men and women, groups have been an avenue, often the only available to us, to self-acceptance. A proliferation of lesbian and gay groups has accompanied the development of our culture. These groups extend beyond gay affirmation to offer support around a range of issues. Many large urban areas, for example, have groups specially set up for gay people of color, gay substance abusers and their partners, parents and children of gays, older lesbians and gays, and other special subgroups. Such groups are advertised in gay and feminist bookstores and rap centers, and in lesbian and gay periodicals.

In less urban areas, gay men and lesbians may find such rap groups unavailable, and must participate in non-gay groups. What they find there varies greatly.

One openly gay man who went to an Alcoholics Anonymous meeting in the midwest said that he was warmly received. The common bond of alcoholism made other differences irrelevant.

Another gay men who went to a regular therapy group in a suburban area said it took him a long time to get over the coming out hurdle. After he said that he was gay, he felt support from most of the group members. But one person made him a target and was abusive. The gay group member interpreted the group leader's failure to intervene on his behalf as being a subtle expression of the leader's own homophobia.

Types of Groups

Groups with Leaders. Groups, like the people who go to them, are all different. Typically, counseling groups consist of six to ten members, and a leader who is usually, but not necessarily, a therapist. Groups can be time-limited, with a specific ending date, or they may continue indefinitely. Sessions usually last for an hour or two and cost less than individual therapy — often between $5 and $40 a session. Groups run by agencies are often free for people who can't afford to pay.

Sometimes group leaders expect monthly payments in advance and do not refund money for missed sessions.

It's important to find out about payment policies. Does the leader intend to raise fees? Will you be charged if you cancel? What if you take a vacation?

Facilitators' styles range from very directive — perhaps working individually with one group member while the rest of the group looks on — to relatively passive, even invisible. Like with individual therapists, the approach taken by group facilitators will vary. Some feel that the expression of feelings is the most important function of the group. Others focus on behavioral change and give "homework" assignments toward that end. Still others may be concerned with correcting distortions in perspective that interfere with interpersonal interactions. Eclectic therapists may combine all three approaches.

In the last ten years, the mega-group, which commonly includes scores or even hundreds of participants, has emerged as a controversial new form. Such groups, frequently marathons, may last for several consecutive days. "Trainers" or leaders orchestrate exercises which typically include fantasy journeys, trust encounters, and various forms of self-presentation to the group. Such experiences tend to be intense and owe much of their confrontational approach to the encounter groups popular in the sixties.

Self-help groups. Self-help groups have been very effective for members who feel stigmatized by the dominant culture. Women, alcoholics and addicts, incest survivors, AIDS patients, ethnic and other disenfranchised minorities have, by forming their own groups, created a microcosm in which they, the outlaws, the mavericks, are insiders. Sometimes such bonding effectively turns cultural norms on their collective ear.

Though self-help groups have no official leaders, often an informal leader or leaders emerge during the course of the group. These group members may earn leadership status in a variety of ways. Perhaps they have been instrumental in starting the group. Maybe they have had more experience with the problems facing group members. Or they may simply be more comfortable in group settings — the most likely candidates for other participants to turn to for direction or advice.

A preordained structure of rotating leadership is often established to counteract this tendency of groups to stratify into different levels of participation and leadership. In the various Anonymous groups (Alcoholics Anonymous, Overeaters Anonymous, Gamblers Anonymous, etc.), for example, meetings are led each time by different members who volunteer to speak on a particular theme, and then help to guide the ensuing discussion. Feminist groups, as well, frequently devise some strategy to be limited to a specific number of responses. Other groups may use time constraints to equalize participation — participants must limit their comments to a few minutes.

Self-help groups are more likely to be open-ended than officially led groups; and consequently, they are easier to sample. They are also likely to be free. Most importantly, they give participants a unique opportunity to sculpt the kind of help they receive.

Some Problems with Groups. Groups aren't for everybody. The most common complaint is the lack of individual attention. It's hard to explore oneself in a thorough way when you're sharing the spotlight with eight or ten or twenty other people.

Groups are also inflexible. They usually meet at a certain time regardless of the scheduling conflicts of any individual member. In contrast to individual therapy, groups, if they are open-ended and have transient membership, may not be able to generate the feeling of stability necessary to make participants feel safe enough to risk personal disclosures.

One woman reported that she simply hated groups. She'd tried several and had always felt uncomfortable. She didn't like to talk in front of people she didn't trust. She was particularly uncomfortable during the silences because of the pressure she felt to say something. Though she was isolated in her life, the group experiences only increased her feeling of isolation. She left most sessions feeling more depressed than usual.

Another woman complained that lesbian groups were cliquey and incestuous. There were always those who were in and those who were out. It felt like high school. Everybody was either cruising or griping about their lovers. She also had doubts about the group's confidentiality, having heard "confidential" group information through the grapevine.

As with individual therapy, a successful group experience depends both on the compatibility of its participants' personalities, and the fit between the group approach and the goals of its members. Awareness of the array of choices and an informed, empowered consumer stance are just as crucial for selecting a group as they are for choosing an individual therapist.

Consumer Considerations. If you're interested in joining a therapy group, how do you find the one that's right for you? Some groups have an open-membership policy, which makes it possible for you to sample different groups on a one-time basis. In groups with closed memberships and groups which are time-limited, drop-in visitors aren't usually welcome. If you're interested in researching such a group, a good way to start is to schedule an interview with the group leader, if there is one. The meeting won't thoroughly convey the feeling of the group, but you'll know a lot about its leader's style.

As significant a factor as the leader is, it's possible that you'll like the leader but not the group. And once you've joined a group you may feel pressure not to drop out. But remember: it's just as important in a group as it is in individual therapy to pay attention to your own needs. Give it a few sessions. If the group still doesn't seem to be what you want, give advance notice that you're leaving, so you'll have time to hear members' reactions.

After trying a group, Tony decided that it wasn't for him. He wanted to quit, but in the two months he'd been coming no one else had left; he felt reluctant to break the unwritten rule. Tony was enormously relieved when a therapist friend told him that part of every group's work was to deal with people coming and going. By leaving, he would give the group members an opportunity to deal with feelings of loss that are an inevitable part of everyone's life. Tony left the group with some sadness but no regrets. And the group survived his departure.

Mix and Match:
Creating Your Own Therapy Combination

Frequently, a combination of more than one type of therapy is what works best:

Arlene felt she had a pattern of self-devaluation. Her early experiences had convinced her that she was worthwhile only insofar as she took care of others. She felt negated in her primary relationship, but kept silent about the anger she frequently felt. Arlene started with an individual counselor, then began alternating solo sessions with couples' therapy. She also enrolled in an assertiveness training group at the local women's center. At one point she was engaged in individual, couples', and group therapy. She felt that each contributed in different ways to changing both her image of herself, and her bevavior.

In our everyday lives, we function in three spheres — as individuals, as participants in relationships, and as members of the larger culture. Each different form of therapy may be useful at different times, in different ways, to highlight different aspects of our identities. Deciding which form of therapy is most appropriate for us is, in itself, a valuable preliminary experience in self-exploration.

—II—
The Nuts and Bolts of Seeking, Negotiating and Evaluating Therapy

——5——
Beginning the Search:
Therapy Types to Choose From

A good place to begin shopping for a therapist is to decide whether you're looking for *public* or *private* therapy; that is, whether you should seek a counselor who practices in a mental health center, clinic or public agency — or a private practitioner.

The public mental health clinic may be a department in a hospital, university or other major institution, or it may be an independent entity. The clinic may have as its targeted population certain groups — geographic, ethnic, collegiate, economically disadvantaged or employees of a particular company or industry. In a few major cities, gay people are among the groups served by such specialized agencies.

In contrast to private practitioners (who depend on their clients for income), the funding for such clinics or agencies usually comes from some combination of government grants, money raised in the local community and client fees. Besides the differences in funding sources, clinics or agencies and private practitioners vary in a number of other significant ways. Because these differences have specific consequences for consumers, they are important to consider.

Public Agencies Versus Private Practitioners

Fees: Most agencies have a sliding fee scale. Depending on your income, you may pay a token fee of a few dollars, on up to fees comparable to those charged by private therapists. The least you can expect to pay a private therapist, in contrast, is around $25. Some do offer sliding scales, but the range of fees is usually higher than those charged in agencies.

Crisis Care: Most clinics, hospitals, and agencies have enough staff to provide both "hot" and "cool" services — that is, help during crises as well as in less-than-urgent situations. For urgent care, they usually have on-duty counselors available on the spot to talk to by phone. Hospital emergency rooms, however, may be the only resource that can provide this kind of service all night. In most cases the person on duty in an emergency room is a member of a rotating team set up to handle emergencies during specified shifts. The counselor you talk to under such circumstances is unlikely to be assigned as your ongoing counselor; more likely he or she will refer you to another counselor in the agency.

If you're seeing a private therapist, he or she will see you through your "hot" situations as well as your "cooler" times. Instead of being treated by an unfamiliar emergency room staffer, you'll have the reassurance of you "own" therapist, and the advantage of your history together — if, of course, the therapist is available at the time of your crisis.

Diversity of Services and Staff: As well as providing individual counseling services, some agencies also offer special groups, seminars, and day programs. Crisis switchboards, groups for coming out, for alcohol and drug problems, or for particular age groups are not uncommon at centers that serve gay populations. Nongay agencies may also offer a variety of groups, educational and recreational activities. Clients of private practitioners may have access to comparable resources through referrals from their therapists.

An agency's staff is likely to offer a variety of backgrounds — a heterogeneity which a therapist in private practice obviously cannot provide. In the course of treatment at a single clinic, a gay Latin man, who was a recovering addict, had contact with: a street worker whose training consisted of his own recovery from drugs plus a one-year program at the local junior college; a psychiatrist who saw him once a week; a bilingual occupational therapist from Nicaragua and a social worker who specialized in vocational rehabilitation.

In contrast to private practitioners, counselors working in an institutional setting do not have to be licensed by the state. They simply have to be supervised by someone with a license. This gives the agency greater latitude in hiring. Some agency counselors will be licensed, others not; some will be hired because they have skills developed through their unique experiences; other counselors will be interns or students working toward a license. This mixture can lend a richness and diversity of treatment, style, and personality that will be useful to the person seeking help.

Loyalty. While private practitioners depend on their clients for income, the salaries of therapists in clinics are paid by the clinic itself. The clinic, in turn, may be funded by federal, state or local governments, foundations, corporations, donations, etc. Unlike a private therapist, employees of such clinics are loyal and accountable primarily to the person or organization that pays their salary. So the goals, and agenda of the agency's administration may take precedence over the client's needs. For example, if the agency's policy is to handle clients on the basis of a short-term crisis intervention only and a client happens to need more than the prescribed six visits, agency policy will usually prevail. Agency counselors may also be negatively influenced by seeing new patients as an additional strain to an already stressful schedule — and this may diminish the quality of care they offer.

Choice of Therapist. If you are shopping for a private therapist, you can choose from the variety of therapists available in your vicinity. You can interview one or two, pick the one that seems most suitable, and switch to a different therapist if the first choice isn't working out. Within an institutional or agency setting, you have a very limited choice of therapists. After an intake interview, clients are usually assigned to the counselor deemed most appropriate by the interviewer or — if the caseloads are heavy — to anyone available at the time. This may or may not produce a good match.

Clients are occasionally able to change therapists within agencies, but such flexibility is limited by several factors. Dissatisfied clients who shift therapists interfere with the smooth working of the agency system and burden the administrators with extra paperwork. In addition, agency therapists who are rejected by clients look bad to their coworkers in the agency. To avoid appearing inadequate or incompetent, they may not support the transfer of a dissatisfied client.

Although *all* clients are entitled to consumer rights, another difference arises from the economics of the situation. Private therapy clients may, by virtue of their "paying customer" status, demand these rights more assertively than agency clients who are paying little or nothing for treatment. A request for a change of therapist may be perceived — by both the therapist and the client — as a lack of gratitude. In other words, agency clients may feel, or be made to feel, that they have no right to complain.

Record-Keeping. Nobody requires that the private practitioners keep logs, notes or records of their sessions. Many don't. In an institution, such record-keeping is evidence that services are being provided. The more client-service hours therapists log, the more likely it is that government and foundation funding will continue. If funding is decreased, jobs are lost.

Record-keeping has its pros and cons for the therapy client. On the plus side, records may help therapists remember past disclosures, thereby providing more complete and continuous pictures of their clients' lives. There are also negatives.

Not infrequently, Social Security numbers are part of the client's record — thus potentially locking the client's particular mental health chart into the national computer net, at the discretion of the agency itself. Should any federal agencies, particularly those concerned with national security, become interested in a client's background, it would not be difficult to obtain these agency records. It would be much harder to gain access to records kept by a private practitioner — assuming such records existed in the first place.

Another problem is that records in public agencies tend to accumulate — stacked up on desks, buried in bottom drawers, or even smuggled out for an evening's catch- up work at home. In fact, most therapists at mental health centers are behind in their paperwork. All of this means that bureaucratic foul-up increases the possibility of misplaced charts, of many people handling and looking at records, of client records being temporarily or permanently lost.

Agency counselors are also required to prepare regular patient assessments, including diagnoses. Such diagnoses can be damning enough to guarantee permanent stigma. Unfortunately for clients, the more serious the diagnosis, the more it helps the agency to justify its funding. After all, if a clinic is treating an unusual number of violent or suicidal patients, the need for continued funding becomes obvious.

Such a situation creates pressure for practitioners, faced with a choice of diagnosis, to opt for the more serious and more stigmatizing assessments. Aside from the diagnosis, and the deficiency it implies, the mere fact that someone is being treated in a mental health agency may be more information than some individuals want divulged about themselves.

In short, the choice of counselor who works in an agency or clinic means certain consumer benefits — low fees, and a broad spectrum of services, for example. The choice of a private practitioner has other positive consequences for the consumer — most significantly, a client-counselor relationship free of bureaucratic constraints.

Because the differences between agencies or clinics, and private practitioners have such an impact on the therapy that consumers receive, the choice is important and deserves particular attention.

Measuring the Effectiveness of Therapy

Whether you're looking for a public or private therapist, you will confront the issue of effective therapy. How can you know if the therapy you receive is worthwhile? Or whether the therapist is competent?

The search for criteria by which to measure this effectiveness has been undertaken with gusto over the last thirty years. As yet this effort has yielded little data the consumer can use. Why haven't researchers been able to come up with some definitive statements about what works and what doesn't in psychotherapy?

One explanation is the dilemma that plagues all social scientists. Research implies measurement; measurement implies strict, undeviating standards. Since no two people are alike, it's difficult to accurately measure and compare a group which has had psychotherapy with a group which hasn't.

If, for instance, the treated group shows improvement, can it be concluded that psychotherapy caused the improvement? Maybe the subjects found more supportive friends. Maybe their problems were less severe than they first appeared to be. Maybe there were external changes — the removal of an oppressive boss or the end of a destructive relationship. And what is the measure of improvement itself? The ability to stay out of jail or the hospital? To get a pay raise? To jog more miles per day? And what if the people closest to the experimental subjects insist that, contrary to the researcher's claim of improvement, the subject is as difficult as ever to live with? Who is right?

The absence of conclusions in the field of psychotherapy leaves a vacuum which graduate schools and licensing boards have attempted to fill. Degrees, typically the first step toward a career as a therapist, are conferred by educational institutions. Licenses, the next step, are awarded by the state. The acquisition of a license usually means that therapists have passed some kind of minimum qualifying examinations, or have met certain requirements set by the state in consultation with professional groups charged with the maintenance of standards and codes. A license permits a therapist to establish a private practice, outside of the supervision required within an institution.

The lack of uniformity among graduate schools and licensing boards robs consumers of the reliability these procedures and policies could promise. There is a great variety among the schools that train therapists. Some are accredited by a state, regional or national professional organization which seeks to maintain uniform, high standards. Others are simply unaccredited schools or diploma mills that require little from students beyond the payment of fees.

In addition to academic credentials, the issue of quality comes up in the licensing procedures implemented by state and professional licensing boards. After being supervised in the practice of psychotherapy for a certain period of time, and passing certain exams, a therapist receives a license to practice independently. Yet there is no clear link between successful completion of such programs or exams and professional competency.

Counselors who have taken licensing exams report that the questions seem arbitrary, often unrelated to their actual practice of psychotherapy. In the preparation courses for such exams, students are often advised to claim a specific theoretical orientation. Those who consider themselves eclectic are warned that they might fail if they base their presentations on the actual therapy methods which they have found work best with their clients. This is true even though many of these students have been working (under supervision) for some time.

There are other reasons to doubt that degrees and licensing automatically vest some special magic in a therapist. In one research study, a group of para-professional counselors without specialized training ranked as high on such attributes as warmth, genuineness and empathy as did seasoned professionals. Ranking far below groups in the study were graduate students and internists in psychology — women and men on the threshold of being licensed.

Finally, graduate schools and the licensing process, if they do not actually reinforce homophobic attitudes, rarely do anything to counteract them. Therapists who are gay often do not feel safe enough to come out in such settings; indeed, the consequences of such exposure may be harmful. One woman in a graduate counseling program was suspected by her advisor of being a lesbian. The advisor announced one day that the student's graduation would be contingent upon her seeing a traditional psychiatrist to "deal with her confused sexuality."

In some states, candidates who reveal a gay sexual orientation are likely to be denied their licenses. Even openly gay candidates who pass the exams frequently report interrogation, bordering on harassment, by examiners about lesbian and gay issues.

Even so, while degrees and licenses may conceal more about the attitudes and competency of counselors than they reveal, they do represent the most common way for differentiating therapists. It is important for consumers to know the general categories of degrees and licenses you can expect to encounter in agencies, clinics, or the private sector:

Degrees
1) The Master's Degree (M.A., M.S., M.S.W.): The largest category of counselors offering private services are those with Master's degrees. Such practitioners have usually had two years of psychological training, which in-

cludes on-the-job experience. Among them, you will find social workers, psychiatric nurses and family counselors.

2) The Ph.D. Degree: This degree requires four years of graduate school, plus a period of supervised internship — usually about two years. Most therapists with a Ph.D degree have earned it in clinical psychology — the specialty dealing with the therapeutic practice of psychology. Although some counselors who are psychologists have Master's degrees, the majority of psychologists in clinical practice have Ph.D.s.

Because of the length of their training period, clinical psychologists are likely to charge higher fees than are recipients of Master's degrees. They are also more likely to be called to testify in court cases, to offer psychological testing services, and to teach.

3) The M.D. Degree: The specialist with a medical degree in the field of mental health is a psychiatrist. Psychiatrists have completed four years of medical school, a year's internship, plus a three-year residency in a psychiatric hospital or other institutional setting. Psychiatrists can prescribe medicine. They are most likely to be heads of clinics and are frequently called upon to give "expert" court testimony.

Licenses

Licensing requirements, categories, and recognition vary from state to state. The ones you are most likely to encounter are:

1) L.C.S.W. (Licensed Clinical Social Worker). Social Work licenses are usually granted by a state board of examiners after the completion of Masters of Social Work degree, and two years of practice supervised by another

licensed social worker, psychologist or psychiatrist. In addition, state laws usually require licensed social workers to pass a written or oral examination.

2) M.A. (Master's Degree in Counseling). There are many regional variations in the title of this degree and its eligibility for licensing. In states where a Counseling Masters can lead to a license, candidates must complete a two-year graduate program, be supervised by a licensed clinician for two subsequent years or for a certain number of specified practice hours, and must pass an exam.

3) Ph.D. (Doctoral degree in psychology). Beyond the completion of a graduate psychology program, licensure candidates must be supervised, usually by a licensed psychologist, for two years or its equivalent in practice hours, and must pass state licensing exams.

4) M.D. (Medical Degree in Psychiatry). In addition to medical school, psychiatrists-in-training must usually complete a year's internship, a three- or four-year psychiatric residency under supervision, and pass the state medical board examinations in order to be licensed.

If you are enrolled in a medical plan that pays, or contributes towards therapy, you'll need to check what level of degree or licensing is required by the insurance company for reimbursement. Eligibility requirements vary from state to state. Some insurance companies will reimburse counselors with Master's degrees; some will not. Federal programs like Medicare/Medicaid will only reimburse treatment supplied by the holder of a Ph.D. or M.D. degree.

Unlicensed Helpers
There are a number of gay-affirmative counselors

who, though unlicensed, offer services that widen the choices facing consumers. Such independent practitioners may label themselves teachers, resource people or consultants. One woman, a group facilitator for years, describes herself as a "teacher of cooperative problem-solving skills." A special degree or license would not enhance her goal of providing consumers with a model of equalized power. "My lack of professional status," she says, "brings me a very appealing group of people to work with."

Another woman, a lesbian feminist, has her number listed in a local feminist directory as a contact person for Fat Liberation. As a result she fell into the role of informal telephone counselor. "Women began calling me for phone advice and consolation. I really like talking to women and hearing their stories. I don't do it because it is some charitable work. I do it because it gives me a charge."

There is one major drawback to unlicensed counselors who work outside the protective jurisdiction of a clinic or agency. If you, as a consumer, are dissatisfied, you have no formal grievance procedures to pursue. Licensed therapists face the threat, if consumer complaints prove legitimate, of revoked licenses. Unless they are masquerading as licensed psychotherapists — or advertising services they are not qualified to provide — unlicensed helpers are relatively immune from legal or professional redress. The combined advantages of a strong consumer orientation and reduced fees may balance the disadvantages of going to an unlicensed helper for counseling.

Although the license does not ensure skill, it is

usually related to the fee you will be charged. Most Master's level counselors who see people privately fall within the $15 to $65 range. It is difficult to find a Ph.D. psychologist who will charge as little as $25; some may, in urban areas, go as high as $100 a session. For psychiatrists the typical rate hovers in the $70 to $80 range and may, in urban areas, exceed $100.

These variations reflect both the experience of the therapists and the regions in which they practice. One woman was paying $20 a session in Louisville, Kentucky. When she moved to the Bay Area, she was taken aback to find therapists with equivalent experience charging twice that much. When she moved again, this time to Los Angeles, she had cause to look back nostalgically at San Francisco. The L.A. equivalent charged $60. All three counselors had Master's degrees and were lesbian therapists with approximately five years' experience.

No direct correlation between degrees of licenses and effectiveness as a therapist has been established. The absence of reliable standards in the field of psychotherapy leads to one conclusion: As consumers, we must bring our own rating system to therapy. Our own evaluation should determine the practitioner and therapeutic approach that works best for us. This same consumer competency can shape our decisions about scheduling, fees, what ground to cover in therapy, what areas *not* to explore, and when to end therapy. In a framework of consumer empowerment, decisions that were once the exclusive domain of the therapist begin to include the judgments of the other expert on the scene: you, the consumer.

6

Finding a Lesbian/Gay Affirmative Therapist

Perhaps the most important quality that lesbians and gay men shop for in a therapist — an affirmative attitude towards our sexuality — is also the most difficult to find. After all, "gay" or "lesbian" is not a single kind of behavior. Each represents a whole cluster of styles, sexual practices, tastes, social environments, and political networks. Obviously, there can be no single, monolithic attitude toward such a behavioral mix on the part of any therapist. And the ways in which such therapists demonstrate gay-affirmative attitudes, as these examples show, can take very different shapes.

Larry. After Larry had been in therapy for two years, his relationship with his lover ended. A Baptist youth group had been Larry's mainstay years before when his parents divorced. Even after he left home and came out, he had gone back to the church periodically. Lonely and bewildered after the breakup, Larry decided to attend services again. At one of the church meetings, he met a man who introduced Larry to his circle of friends — all members of a group of formerly gay men who were attempting to practice Christian teachings by honoring the Biblical injunctions against homosexuality. Still unhappy about the dissolution of his relationship, Larry joined the group.

Larry's counselor, Eric, found that he could not listen passively to Larry's accounts of his new direction. During the months that Larry went to the Christian group, Eric continued to offer him a perspective which affirmed the expression of his sexuality. When Larry fully renounced his gayness, Eric said he could no longer be comfortable or effective working with Larry. He felt Larry's choice was based on the suppression of much of what was important and satisfying to Larry and was therefore not a healthy one. Eric said he could not support Larry in a course he felt was damaging; he advised Larry to find a counselor who could be supportive of his decisions.

Torrie. Torrie, who was heterosexual, had several close friends in the advertising company for which she worked. One was a lesbian who had been out for years. Another woman had recently declared herself gay. The three women often had lunch together, and occasionally Torrie would go to parties at their homes. At one party, Torrie met Nina. They realized immediately that they had a lot in common and Nina found Torrie attractive. After they had gone to the movies together a few times, Nina proposed they sleep together.

Torrie didn't know what to do. She had no moral objections to sex with a woman, but she was confused. She felt warm, but not passionate toward Nina. With some misgivings, Torrie made an appointment with a psychiatrist recommended by her friends at work. When she found out the psychiatrist was openly gay, she was afraid she would be pressured into a premature choice — recruited into a lesbian lifestyle.

During the first session, Torrie made a point to describe the passionate sex she had recently had with a man. She watched for the therapist's reaction. Interest, concern — nothing else. Then she talked about her warm feelings toward Nina and said she had decided to sleep with Nina — which was, at that point, untrue. Again Torrie scrutinized the therapist. The same interest, warmth — nothing more. She repeated this test several times during the early sessions.

Later, they talked about it. Torrie had expected the therapist to be a gung-ho, flag-waving lesbian, eager to encourage same-sex encounters in her clients. The therapist hadn't fit her expectations. Eventually satisfied that the therapist had no vested interest in her feelings, Torrie was able to discuss them candidly.

Torrie and Larry's therapists were very different. Both were gay-affirmative. Torrie's therapist believed that affirmation, on her part, meant supporting Torrie no matter what her sexual direction might be. And Larry's therapist felt he could not be authentic if he did not challenge Larry and eventually refer him elsewhere.

There is no single profile of a gay-affirmative therapist. Such therapists, like any other counselors, run the gamut of experience and training. "Gay-affirming" simply represents an additional layer on top of their particular therapy orientation. Such therapists share a determination not to reinforce in gay and lesbian clients the devaluing messages issuing from the culture. Instead, they offer clients the view that being lesbian or gay is a positive choice.

Not all these therapists are themselves lesbian or gay. In some parts of the country, lesbian or gay therapists may be difficult, even impossible, to find. In such areas, you may be lucky to find a heterosexual therapist who is supportive. There's no rule that says a heterosexual therapist can't be helpful to us — and none that promises competence and nurturing from a therapist who is gay.

Your own instincts, because they are the best guide to the effectiveness of any therapist, deserve attention and respect. In addition, there are some ways of supplementing your intuition — clues which, if observed, will maximize your chances of finding gay-affirmative therapy.

How to Check a Counselor's Attitude

Obviously, a referral is the fastest — and least risky — way to meet a gay-affirmative therapist. When there's no such referral, and no other evidence is forthcoming — no gay periodicals in the waiting room and no clearly affirmative statements from the counselor — you need to look for subtler clues.

How does the therapist say your lover's name? What expressions and body language do you notice when you describe something sexually explicit? How does the coun-

selor react to words like "dyke" and "faggot?" How does
the counselor respond when you discuss AIDS or becoming a gay or lesbian parent?

Invisibility is part of the problem facing any lesbian
or gay man who goes to therapy. An important aspect of
the treatment will be the positive quote marks the therapist puts around lesbian and gay experiences. By asking
questions that provoke openness and elaboration on the
part of the client, the therapist says, "Your life has validity. You exist."

If the therapist is not affirmative about lesbian and
gay experiences, it will be difficult to help the client
become and remain so. The focus of work with gay clients
is to flush out the old, demeaning standards and hold
them up for examination. It means helping the client
realize the inapplicability and irrelevance of many non-
gay values. A therapist who has any doubt, hesitation or
ambivalence about this is probably the wrong one for you;
such a therapist may only reinforce the homophobia that
is inside and around you. In the absence of any clear-cut
statements by your therapist, your intuition is probably
your best guide. Use it.

On the subject of finding a gay-affirmative therapist,
one clinical psychologist has this to say:

"Please pay attention to your intuitions. Do you feel
good being in the room with this person? Do you feel the
person understands what you're talking about? If you have
a negative response, if there is a question in your mind
about what's causing the negative response, for God's sake
ask a question and measure the response. If you're not

sure whether or not your therapist is gay and you want to know, *ask*."

Some therapists will answer forthrightly. Some will question your reasons for wanting to know. Some will refuse point-blank to discuss it. What's most important for you to evaluate is your therapist's level of comfort with the subject. An emphatic negative response, for instance, may be a red flag of warning for you.

Shopping for a Bi-focal Approach

Gay-affirmation is an indispensable part of effective therapy with lesbians and gay men. Good therapy, however, is not limited to lesbian and gay issues. Plenty of problems, although they may be indirectly related to sexual orientation, have a reality independent of lesbianism or gayness. Such problems, which must be dealt with separately, include: drug or alcohol abuse; parenting or career issues; aging; and illness.

Thus, we can say that a gay or lesbian counselor, to be most effective, must have a bi-focal approach, an ability to move easily from a gay perspective to one where homosexuality is incidental. A therapist without this ability can do limited good. Such a therapist may overidentify with a client, flatten the differences among clients, rob each client of her or his uniqueness and provide too limiting or too comforting an environment.

Although she hated her secretarial job, BeaJay was depressed when she was laid off. Going through the masquerade of heels and makeup necessary for a job search seemed unbearable. Rather than start the search, she began spending her afternoons at the lesbian bars, shooting pool. She was usually drunk by the time she came home for dinner. Alarmed at her personality change, her lover insisted that she go to a clinic. BeaJay agreed.

BeaJay spent the next three months discussing her previous coming out struggles and her current objections to a closeted lifestyle with a sympathetic counselor. The therapist shared BeaJay's perceptions of a hostile world and rankled with the same sense of unjustice. Meanwhile, BeaJay started going to the bars more frequently and staying there till later at night. She began to miss her therapy appointments; eventually, she stopped going completely. She was too hungover to get up for morning sessions.

When her lover left six months later, BeaJay went to another counselor. After questioning her, the counselor said that her reasons for coming — being a lesbian in a straight world, her lover's departure — were secondary to BeaJay's real problem: alcoholism. She agreed to work with BeaJay if she entered an alcohol treatment program.

Gay-affirming therapy means active opposition to homophobia. It does not mean, in the process, that the therapist loses sight of each client's individuality or the uniqueness of the dilemmas each client faces.

Of course, the concept "gay-affirming" does not mean straight therapists cannot be effective with lesbian and gay clients. But it may be difficult, sensitive as we are to the possibility of homophobia, to assess nongay therapists fairly. For instance, a gay therapist may comment, make an interpretation, or pass judgment in a way that seems acceptable, while the same remarks, coming from a straight therapist, would sound antigay.

One lesbian client remarked, "I would complain, say something negative about the lesbian community. I might say it was too incestuous and think nothing of it. But when my straight therapist would say the same thing back to me, just paraphrasing what I'd said, I would think she was being homophobic and judgmental."

The only solution to this is to make homophobia a *visible* partner in treatment. Keep the subject open with the therapist. Homophobia in ourselves as well as in others is always dangerous, but it is particularly lethal when it goes underground.

Terrified about the recent emergence of his gay feelings, a man who worked as an executive in a large corporation returned to the psychiatrist who had helped him through a divorce several years before. Noting that the visit coincided with the anniversary of the final divorce decree, the therapist concluded that his former patient was depressed, and prescribed medication. The homosexual feelings, he said, were part of the depression and would dissipate when the medication took effect. More depressed than ever after the session, the patient struggled with suicidal feelings for days, on the verge of overdosing with the prescribed drugs.

Far less visible in this situation, yet just as problematic as the client's depression, was the therapist's (and client's) homophobia. Because it was unmentioned and unattended, it transformed an emotional problem into a life-threatening crisis.

How to Find a Gay-Affirmative Therapist

Bookstores, Coffeehouses, Newspapers. These will often provide leads through bulletin boards, conversations or advertisements.

Lesbian/gay newsletters, journals, flyers and newspapers carry ads like the following, offering a profusion of approaches and reflecting a variety of backgrounds:

LESBIAN FEMINIST THERAPIST

I am an experienced lesbian-feminist therapist. I work with individuals and couples. Techniques I have found useful derive from Gestalt Therapy, Transactional Analysis and Hypnotherapy. Counseling as I practice it aims at self-understanding, self-education. My fee ranges from $20 to $50. Open to bartering. M.S., M.F.C.C.

THERAPY FOR GAY MEN

Lack of Intimate Relationships
Low Self-Esteem
Overcoming Shyness
AIDS Crisis Issues
Building Sturdy Relationships
I accept Medi-cal and insurance. First session free.

MINORITY COUNSELING

I am a black Lesbian, a supportive and confrontive therapist, who respects each person's unique sense of timing and readiness. I work especially with issues of inti-

macy, independence, power, sexuality,
racism and classism. Sliding Scale. Ph.D.

EXPERIENCED M.D.
Help for individuals in crisis and for persons
seeking positive change who are experiencing stress and life transition difficulties. I
specialize in sex therapy, gender counseling,
for couples and singles. Psychological testing
is available.

Ads are a legitimate way to find a therapist. Some offer
initial consultations free — a good way to start the shopping process. Many therapists who don't advertise free
first sessions will offer one if you ask.

Lesbian/Gay Community Leaders. Brian wanted to find a
gay-affirming therapist on the staff of a city clinic serving
his district. He called several local high-profile gay men
and lesbians. None of them knew anyone in the clinic he
had targeted, but they provided several leads. One was a
lesbian who had done volunteer work on a local mental
health committee. She gave Brian the name of a sympathetic therapist who worked in the clinic.

Another source of leads to counselors who work in
agencies or clinics are lesbian or gay private practitioners.
Therapists often know each other through personal or professional networks.

Switchboards. Operating in many urban areas, switchboards provide a source of lesbian/gay counselors. They

are usually listed in the phonebook under "Feminist," "Gay," "Lesbian," or "Women." In areas without visible gay or feminist communities, switchboards for crisis intervention, substance abuse support, or even peace groups may offer the information you need.

Lesbian and Gay Directories. The professional organizations to which psychotherapists belong frequently have lesbian and gay caucuses, which offer, upon request, listings of lesbian and gay therapists across the country. Several other directories for lesbians and gay men also list lesbian and gay mental health resources. See the Resource Section of this book for details.

Sleuthing. The difficulty of finding a gay-affirmative therapist is compounded by closetry — the conviction on the part of some therapists (particularly those who work in agencies or clinics) that they dare not come out at work. A social worker in a mental health clinic in Dallas described his dilemma.

"I cannot come out. My coworkers, who are homophobic, would treat me differently. They would withdraw their respect and confidence and I would be socially isolated. It's particularly agonizing to me when gay clients come to the clinic asking for a gay therapist. I can't request that these clients be assigned to me without arousing suspicion."

Despite this therapist's desire to be helpful, he feels limited by his homophobic work environment. Thousands of lesbian/gay counselors across the country are similarly entombed in their professional closets.

One lesbian client used a particularly creative strategy to ferret out just such a closeted therapist. She strode purposefully into a nearby psychiatric clinic, which was part of a larger hospital complex. She told the receptionist that she was a member of a committee that the hospital had established to investigate the implementation of sexual harassment laws in the hospital. Was there anyone in the clinic, interested in feminist issues, who might be recruited for the committee? The receptionist gave her the name of a social worker. The woman called the social worker and asked if she could circumvent the usual intake procedures to see her. It turned out to be a good match.

If you get the name of someone in a clinic, call the person directly. If the person is lesbian or gay and closeted, a comment like "you've been recommended to me as a therapist and I want to know if I can arrange to be seen by you," is a nonthreatening introduction. Approached in this way, therapists will often either arrange to see you, or alert the intake worker to assign you to him or her.

Lesbians and gays have special mental health care needs that require extra persistence and commitment on the consumer's part. But the reward of finding the right therapist and having a positive therapy experience makes the search worthwhile.

Country Ways

Many of America's gay people live far from urban centers: in small towns; on farming collectives; or with their parents. Often the prevailing homophobia keeps rural gays deeply closeted; in other areas, there is more tolerance. Although the task of finding a good therapist is more difficult in such situations, a broader view of your needs will help.

Counseling in the city and in the country look very different. Going to an office for an hour and not seeing the therapist again until the next visit is not country rhythm. And a gay or lesbian identity means something different whether you are closeted or openly gay in the country. You and your neighbor may not see eye to eye on things. Yet you may need to work together — hauling gravel for a road that leads to both your properties, or voting together at a town meeting. As a rural lesbian or gay man, you may be interdependent with people who would not be your intimates in the city.

The task for rural gay people seeking therapy is different from their urban counterparts. When there are no practicing lesbian or gay therapists nearby, how do you find someone who — even if not lesbian or gay — is sympathetic, warm, and supportive? Such a search means getting involved in aspects of local community work which reflect shared values, and cultivating friendships with people who have the qualities you would seek in any therapist. Such people are "natural helpers": those whose listening ability, tolerance, and empathy make them sought-out "counselors" within their communities.

Sukey, a lesbian, was weary of life in L.A. She packed up herself and her ten-year-old son, sold her house, and bought a trailer and fifteen acres in the Pacific Northwest. Sukey intended to be self-sufficient, grow her own food. She became active in the local antinuclear group and the

National Women's Political Caucus. In the process, Sukey met Carol, an activist with whom she felt particular rapport. Sukey started confiding in her.

Sukey noticed that other neighbors also dropped in frequently — probably, she speculated, to confide their problems as she often did. Soon she realized that Carol was a counselor, although she had no degree. Her payment was likely to be a dozen eggs or some goat's milk cheese. Had anyone suggested she was a counselor, Carol would have scoffed at the idea. She was just being neighborly.

When There is No Gay-Affirmative Therapist Nearby

Some rural lesbians and gay men have located therapists in nearby cities whom they drive to see.

If driving long distances for therapy is not feasible, country dwellers may elect, instead, to have telephone therapy. Some therapists who live in urban areas are open to negotiating regular telephone sessions with clients who don't have access to their offices.

Social contact with other lesbians and gay men who are not necessarily counselors may be especially important for rural lesbians and gay men.

The search for a lesbian/gay-affirmative therapist may be quick and direct, or arduous and time-consuming. The search will be facilitated by drawing on available resources; referral sources, national publications; assertive interview techniques, and most importantly, your own creativity and intuition.

——7——
Beginning Therapy

Shopping for a therapist is not a pleasant task; it can be tedious and time-consuming. Nor is it foolproof. One client complained that therapists she'd known had always put their best foot forward during first interviews. After she'd been "hooked," they'd show their true — and very different — colors.

In spite of the hardships involved — the time and the money expenditures, and the unreliability of an assessment based on one or two visits — shopping is well worth the effort. At the very least it gives consumers some basis for comparison, and the opportunity to rehearse the role of interviewer/evaluator. At best, it can save thousands of dollars and hundreds of hours spent with therapists who for one reason or another are not the best for you.

Making That First Call
Calling a therapist or clinic for the first time is

usually an ordeal. After bracing yourself, it seems anti-
climactic to be confronted by an answering machine, or a
switchboard operator who's trying to field four calls at
once. Most therapists are not immediately available by
phone. The time between a call placed and a call returned
may be as little as an hour; more frequently, it's a day or
two. Clients who are anxious about undertaking therapy
in the first place are often relieved by the delay. To those
who feel they're hanging by the fingernails from the for-
tieth floor ledge, even a slight delay in the time the therapist takes to return the first call may seem interminable.

One person reports, "I'd spent the past ten years of my
life lying about being an addict and an alcoholic. I was
scared to go see someone. I was also desperate. Nothing in
my life was working anymore. I called for help — the
phone rang and rang. Finally, a message from an answering machine came on saying everyone in the center was in
a staff meeting and I should call back in the afternoon. I
hung up and didn't call back for six weeks."

The Call-Back
One woman reported that her first phone contact
shaped her subsequent reactions to the therapist. An
assistant answered and told her all of Dr. Schur's rules.
The formality clashed with her style, and because it re-
vealed something about the way the therapist worked —
his style — she did not expect to like him.

When she went for the first appointment, he gave her
a pad and pencil and told her to list some positive things
about her life on one side, and negatives on the other. He
left the room while she completed the list. The exercise

had a mechanical feeling to it. She resented paying for someone's time when he wasn't present. Her experience confirmed her initial impression; she stopped seeing Dr. Schur and continued shopping for another therapist.

Call-back styles vary. Some therapists give little more than the time and address for the initial session during the first call. They prefer to talk about problems, fees and other concerns in person. Other therapists do a complete screening on the phone.

One psychiatric social worker asked first callers several questions: how they had been referred; if they had been in therapy before; what they were looking for in a therapist; why they wanted therapy at this particular time. This counselor screens on the phone because she works in her home and feels cautious about whom she agrees to see. By doing this, she also keeps clients from having to make a trip to her office and spend money and time to find out that she doesn't offer what they want.

Another therapist reported that he actually conducts the first session over the phone. In a twenty minute conversation, he establishes rapport; the transition to the actual session thus becomes easier.

How flexible or formal, how responsive, how busy, how structured, how disclosing, all are stylistic qualities which the therapist makes evident in this first exchange. Future exchanges may confirm the accuracy of your first impressions. On the other hand, first impressions will not always accurately predict what is to come. One woman reported being very uncomfortable during an agency intake procedure. She had to answer an extensive questionnaire about drug-taking and sign a contract. By the time she got to the counselor's office, she was very dubious about the prospect of therapy. In contrast to the impersonal process she had gone through, though, the counselor herself proved to be very human and sympathetic.

Some people report that the first call to the therapist is the beginning, middle and end of therapy. One woman said she felt so much relief after calling the therapist that she decided she could get over any hurdle. By making the dreaded call, she'd proved to herself that she could do it on her own, that she no longer needed therapy. She called back and cancelled.

A man said making the appointment plunged him into an intense review of his life. Reasons for some of his patterns became clear, and he decided he didn't need therapy after all.

Waiting Lists

Therapists with here-and-now approaches usually don't have waiting lists. If they're too busy to schedule an appointment, they will refer you to a less busy therapist. If you want to interview a therapist who does suggest a waiting list, ask if he or she will call you for an initial appointment if another client cancels. Most therapists have a couple of cancellations every week. If you can get to an appointment on short notice, you'll get a chance to sample this therapist's style and decide if he or she is worth waiting for.

First Impressions

One woman became completely disoriented on the

way to her first therapy session. She got on the uptown subway when she was supposed to be going downtown. When she finally got on a downtown train, she got off at the wrong stop. When she arrived at last, the therapist's office building, which had the same grimy brick facade as every other building on the block, stood out unnaturally — almost magically. She didn't know if it really looked different or if, in her nervous state, she was attributing strange auric qualities to uninspired, municipal architecture.

It's hard to feel serene on the first trip to a new therapist. And it's even harder not to have strong feelings about the place the therapist works in. Institutional-looking buildings are likely to evoke one set of associations, offices in cozy converted townhouses or Victorians another, and sleek offices with the posh-doctor look still another.

One woman whose therapist worked at home was happy with the informal setting. She liked the fact that the therapist's overstuffed chairs looked as though they had been recycled several times. It lessened the professional distance between the two of them.

A man whose psychologist's office was in his home had a different reaction. He didn't want to know so much about his therapist. He didn't approve of the beer and Tab cans overflowing the garbage can, or the fact that the therapist subscribed to a tabloid that the client thought was trashy.

Waiting rooms are also rich in associations. They evoke memories of waiting to be pronounced well or ill by doctors who often inflict pain, evaluate and perhaps lecture you. One woman who'd spent much of her childhood in doctors' offices getting allergy shots noticed that she automatically started hyperventilating whenever she entered a waiting room. It didn't matter if she was waiting for an attorney or a counselor or a veterinarian — she still relived the old childhood experiences. Such powerful impressions don't dissolve easily — though they may be modified by how much or how little the waiting room resembles the torture antechambers of childhood.

One client reported being so anxious at his first appointment — he had put off therapy for seven years — that he was numb. Though he picked up a magazine and flipped through the pages, he had no idea what he was seeing. The receptionist called his name several times before he heard her.

Another client noticed at the moment when he went up to the reception desk that the television in the corner of the waiting room just happened to be broadcasting some news about a gay day at a local amusement park. The gay world had entered the institution. Though the client hadn't been aware of feeling uncomfortable before, he was suddenly aware of feeling much more relaxed.

Evidences of gayness in the waiting room are not necessarily reassuring. One therapist who had an office in the gay part of town and worked primarily with gay clientele had a number of gay periodicals strewn around his waiting room. One of his closeted clients, afraid of being spotted in the neighborhood, hurried into the waiting room and tried to make himself inconspicuous by hiding behind the pages of an emphatically nongay periodical.

A woman whose therapist worked in an agency always went to therapy five minutes late so she wouldn't have to wait in the agency waiting room. She couldn't identify, she said, with the leather dykes and the pre-operative transsexuals waiting to be seen.

First Contact

One man went through everything in his closet before his first therapy session, trying on every possible outfit and then discarding it because it only represented one facet of his personality. He wanted to be perceived, at least by one person in the world, as a whole, unfragmented person. He finally settled halfheartedly on jeans and a polo shirt. He sat through the first session distressed to think that the therapist would see him as frivolous (the polo shirt was mauve) or that he was trying to "butch it up" (the jeans).

A woman who thought she was fat subsisted on diet cola and celery sticks for two days before she saw her therapist for the first time. She spent the initial session trying to ignore the smells coming from the pizza stand across the street, and apologizing for the clamor coming from her midsection.

When self-presentation to a new therapist goes awry, it can be painful enough to raise shudders months later. Mixed in with the pain is also a great deal of information about who you are, who you are not, and who you wish you were. It provides enough to chew on for the first session, and probably many more sessions to come.

As the hungry woman observed months later, her initial self-image problem was the theme which echoed in one form or another all through her therapy — the conflict between accepting or rejecting herself.

The client's initial reactions to the therapist are no less rich in information. According to one research survey, clients prefer a therapist who dresses slightly more formally than they. One woman reported, however, being delighted with a lesbian therapist who wore overalls and workshirts. She said, "After years of sitting on leather couches feeling alienated from male shrinks who looked like they just stepped out of the pages of *Gentlemen's Quarterly*, it was an enormous relief to find someone who looked and dressed sort of like me."

Don felt immediately uneasy the first time he met Aaron, his counselor. He also noticed that he himself was acting deferentially. He was assuming a one-down position he didn't usually take with strangers. Don realized then that Aaron reminded him of the men who'd had the most authority in his life — his father, scoutmaster, high school basketball coach — around whom he had felt particularly powerless. He saw then that some of the characteristic strength he mustered for new situations actually masked some of the old feelings of powerlessness. This was for him an important revelation, and helped explain the uneasiness he felt toward a new "boss" — the counselor.

Initial impressions can also be positive. One woman reported instant rapport with her therapist before a word was uttered. When she examined her reaction more closely, she said it was the therapist's ample body and breasts which made her feel at home. Her grandmother, who'd had a similar kind of body, had rocked her on her lap while they watched television during long winter evenings in Vermont. The client had come to associate full-bodied older women with love and comfort.

What the Therapist Will Think

Because most therapists are sensitive to the cues from which they can construct profiles of prospective clients, they are likely to form immediate impressions of shoppers who ask questions and assume an evaluative stance. Consumers' questions may trigger unfavorable interpretations: the client is resistant; the client is trying to control therapy. And the client's questions may not get answered.

One woman who had been in traditional therapy for years found the idea of interviewing the therapist laughable. "I can just see it. I would go in with paper and pen poised and ask her questions which of course she wouldn't answer. Meanwhile, *she'd* be furiously scribbling notes about the psychological significance of the questions I'd asked. And so it would go. I would leave with a blank sheet and she would have gotten volumes out of the interview."

Despite the risk of coming away empty-handed or of creating an unfavorable impression, it is worthwhile to interview prospective therapists. If the therapist is competent, such questions will result in a sounder, more balanced relationship for ongoing therapy. If the therapist's response doesn't satisfy you, chances are that her or his therapy won't either.

You'd Better Shop Around

There are lots of reasons why a particular therapist may not be the right one for you. Many therapists are homophobic. Other, although gay-affirming, may be a bad match for other reasons: uncongenial style or temperament; differences in age, gender, appearance, or background. All of these factor may contribute to incompatibility between therapist and client and often result in mismatches.

Unfortunately it is hard to assess a mismatch. There is no list of product features ready to be checked. There is no "Consumer Beware" sticker in the waiting rooms. Nor do most consumers have the kind of diverse and multiple therapy experiences needed to provide a basis for comparison shopping.

Although there are limits to the number of therapists one can assess before choosing one, specific questions asked during initial, evaluative sessions can provide the consumer with enough information to diminish the chance of a bad choice. Questions may cover such matters as fees, policy, appointment times, cancellations, emergencies, attitudes toward homosexuality, and training and licensing.

The Shopping List given earlier in this book provides some guidelines for this process. But the most important element in shopping or sampling is *your own* attitude. You do have some measure of control over what happens. Although the stress or pain which led you to the therapist's office in the first place may make you feel things are unmanageable, you have certain things working in your behalf if you put them to work for you. They include your own resolve about what you want; your flexibility in choosing a therapist; your options to refuse or reject an incompatible therapist; your freedom to negotiate fees, times, methods.

Rachel's story is an example of both the obstacles and benefits of being an assertive therapy shopper.

Rachel: One Shopper's Story

Rachel had been unable to formulate an exact picture of her ideal therapist before she went to the family service agency. The counselor assigned to her seemed sensitive and warm. Yet after the session, Rachel went home feeling uncertain. What was wrong? Why hadn't she been swept off her feet as she had expected to be? What *had* she expected? Could she ask for another therapist? But what reasons could she give?

She talked over her dilemma with her roommate, who was in a graduate counseling program. She advised Rachel that it was legitimate to ask for someone else. Rachel called the intake worker at the agency and said she wanted to interview another therapist. The intake worker seemed reluctant to make such a change and told her to talk it over with the first therapist.

Calling back the first therapist was awkward. She wanted to know the reasons for Rachel's dissatisfaction. Haltingly, Rachel said that she just hadn't felt the kind of rapport she had hoped for. The therapist asked if Rachel would come in and talk about it some more. It was difficult for Rachel to say that she was quite certain she wanted to see someone else, but she did so. In chilled tones, the therapist told her she would see what she would do. After some delay, Rachel was assigned to a new therapist, a woman whose style, she felt, was more compatible with her needs.

As thorough as you may be in your explorations of therapists' styles and policies, your ultimate choice of a therapist may be intuitive. We are accustomed to believing that our choices are legitimate only if they are grounded in logic. Our feelings produce decisions that are often as good, if not better than those based on reason, yet we tend to distrust the intuitive process.

If Rachel had been able to identify a specific reason for disliking the first therapist, she might have felt more comfortable saying she wanted someone else. It is important for consumers to remember that an intuitive response to a therapist *is*, in the context of a therapist search, a reasonable response. Trust it.

——8——
Making A Match

The Assertive Consumer

There are infinite variables built into the therapy situation. And there are numerous criteria for gauging the effectiveness of therapy: research studies; the therapist's credentials; and the therapy consumer, who is the most trustworthy judge of her or his own therapy experience.

As consumers, we are constantly assessing our therapy experiences. It is often difficult, however, for us to have enough faith in our own evaluations to look beyond the diplomas or credentials, or the recommendations of friends. We may feel that our own vulnerability in this situation makes us incapable of evaluating a therapist in a face-to-face exchange.

Years ago, Jenny had made what she considered a terrible match. She'd gone to a psychoanalyst, who had uttered no more than ten words during the year she had seen him. She considered the whole episode a waste of time and money. The next time she considered therapy, Jenny promised herself a more careful selection process. She would, she decided, spend more time interviewing — and eliminating — those prospective therapists who didn't seem compatible. When the time came, Jenny began to formulate a series of questions designed to elicit the preliminary information she needed to make a decision. Suddenly she realized that her determination was eroding. She was, after all, quite vulnerable. Her life was out of synch; that was why she wanted therapy in the first place. How could she, under the circumstances, feel competent to judge a therapist?

Despite her misgivings, Jenny made an appointment with Dr. Osawa, a psychologist recommended by a friend. The new counselor's office, with its aura of professionalism, increased her sense of powerlessness. Feeling strained and self-conscious, Jenny began reeling her questions as soon as she sat down: What was Dr. Osawa's approach? Did she believe in taking an active stance with her clients? What was her experience working with lesbians? Had she been in practice a long time?

"It's anxiety provoking to come to therapy," Dr. Osawa responded, "and your questions reflect your anxiety. They're valid questions, and I'll be glad to answer them. But first, I'd like to know why you've come."

Jenny realized Dr. Osawa was right. She *was* anxious. She'd wanted to appear self-possessed, to seem in charge of the situation. She'd expected to come away from the session with plenty of data about the therapist, and nothing more. Jenny made a quick decision to follow Dr. Osawa's agenda. An hour later, she left the office with both the information she wanted about the therapist, as well as a bonus: Dr. Osawa had responded to her feelings as well as her questions. Jenny felt she had been understood and responded to on several levels.

Jenny was fortunate. She found a good therapist. The search was short because, despite her discomfort, she articulated her needs at the beginning of the process. The therapist's response gave her the data she needed to make a decision.

Therapists' Characteristics

A gay-affirmative philosophy is one part — albeit an indispensable part — of a good therapist's approach. There are many other variables — differences in style, background, and experience, for example — that may affect compatibility between client and therapist. The following counselor attributes weigh most heavily in consumers' final selections.

"Way Back When" or "Here and Now." Some therapists rely heavily on historical information about the client's past. Some work exclusively in the here and now. Some think it is valuable to explore early childhood experiences; others see no point in rummaging around in them. This difference in orientation is partly a matter of theory, partly a matter of professional style. Both orientations can be successful.

Ray went into therapy because he was having rows with his lover. The therapist began by exploring Ray's relationship with his brothers and sisters, paying particular attention to the fact that Ray was born seven years after his older brother. His mother's pregnancy term and delivery were also explored. This approach seemed totally useless to Ray and he decided to stop therapy.

In contrast, a woman who was having similar problems with her lover firmly believed that her childhood held the key to her deteriorating relationship. She ended therapy when she realized that her counselor did not care to help her delve deeply into her past.

Interestingly, styles of therapist and client need not match in order to be compatible. One client, whose own style and temperament were very practical and present-focused, appreciated her therapist's more historical orientation. She had never thought of her present problems in light of the past, and it gave her new material to consider.

Experience. Some therapists are relatively new at the business of counseling; others have been practicing for years. Most clients prefer to see seasoned professionals. But such matches don't necessarily work. One man who went to a well-known older therapist was disappointed. He felt he was one of a long parade of clients stretching back through the years; that long ago the therapist had worn out his ability to view his clients' problems with a fresh perspective. The result was a pseudo-authenticity, responses that pretended to be sincere, but were actually well-rehearsed. The client was much happier with his second therapist, a recent graduate, who was often awkward and unpolished. The consumer felt that in this relationship there existed the possibility of some new discoveries, some surprises. In addition there was the matter of the fee. The newly licensed therapist charged less than half as much as the more experienced counselor.

The Ethnic Match. Aside from pairing lesbian and gay clients with lesbian and gay therapists, there are other forms of pairing — gender, race, age, cultural and political background. It is not unusual for a client who is physically challenged to want to work with a therapist who has experienced something similar. One woman who grew up as a red diaper baby in a working-class Jewish family felt she would be most comfortable with a counselor of similar background. A 49-year-old man felt strongly that he wanted a therapist who had weathered the aging crisis. His problem, he felt, was to accept growing old — something he felt no "kid" could help him with

Whether it is wise to choose a therapist who closely matches your own distinguishing characteristics is a controversial matter in the therapy profession. A number of therapists — many of them white and male — do not endorse such pairings. According to David Brenner, author of *The Effective Psychotherapist*, a client who makes a decision based on such considerations must be questioned carefully in the first session. "A person who chooses a therapist in this way may be making other important, personal decisions in an equally superficial manner," Brenner writes.

Eric Erickson, a psychologist who has long earned the wrath of feminists for his interpretations of children's block-building patterns (little boys, Erickson avers, build towers; little girls build enclosed spaces) also discounts an emphasis on subcultural identities. Such identification, he says, is nothing more than "aggravated self-consciousness."

Some minority therapists and some feminist therapists cite reasons why pairings of clients and counselors from similiar backgrounds make sense. White, middle-class, heterosexual standards, they say, have been "normal" for too long. Behavior that doesn't adhere to these standards has been labeled abnormal and wrong for centuries. Matching a client with a therapist who shares certain important characteristics will help the client overcome the bias of the dominant culture. The treatment will neutralize or at least "frame" the value system which has caused some of the trouble in the first place.

Meddlers versus Neutrals. Some therapists are born meddlers — full of directions, suggestions, advice. Others will not give a bit of advice or the slightest hint of opinion. Different clients respond differently to these approaches. Some seek direct intervention in their lives; others like a more neutral position.

Kay, for example, felt initially frustrated by her therapist's refusal to give her advice; later she decided that this nonintervention worked best for her. Kay came to understand that she had characteristically solicited advice from people whom she saw as powerful, simply in order to defy it. This, she realized, was her favorite way of getting her own power. Had her therapist acceded to Kay's demands to "say something concrete," Kay would in fact have gotten much less help than she ended up getting.

Jargon. For some therapists, part of the healing process means isolating and labeling certain behaviors. It is a way of getting a handle on certain problematic parts of ourselves or our lives. Particular schools of therapy have specific names which are used in this process of conceptualization.

A client in one school of therapy describes this process: "I tend to be very critical and contemptuous of people whom I think are ignorant. In the course of therapy, we decided to call this part of myself my Pig Parent. One of our goals was to get my Pig Parent to pipe down."

Other therapists feel it is counterproductive to invent vocabularies or borrow them ready-made from any particular school of therapy. They go out of their way to reflect their clients' own terminology and to delete any phrases which smack of psychologizing. The use of any language that is not used naturally by the client, they maintain, creates unnecessary distance between therapist and client.

Personal Disclosure. Clients react in different ways to self-disclosures by their therapists. One man reported that the most he ever found out about his therapist in five years was his home address — and that only because it was on the mailing label of a magazine in the waiting room. One week after he mentioned it to the therapist, he found that the labels were torn off all the magazines in the office.

Two women who went to a lesbian-feminist therapist

had very different reactions to her. One woman said it was enormously helpful to hear that the therapist was going through hard times in her personal life; it made her human and accessible. The other woman felt used because the therapist spent part of the hour talking about her own problems with her lover.

Touch. Some therapists are formal; their personal style may preclude touching. Others may feel comfortable holding clients during sessions, giving hugs or even massages.

Touching can be delightful, or invasive. One woman who was crying during a session reported feeling distracted when her therapist came over and put an arm around her. She felt as though she was expected to respond and her expression of grief was interrupted. Another man said the only reason he sat through an hour of talk was for the big hug his therapist gave him at the end of his session. That, he said, was what *really* helped him.

Differences in the Perception of the Problem. Some therapists attribute problems to external circumstances: class, race, homophobia, or specific bad experiences. Others believe that external circumstances merely trigger the deep-seated feelings that are the real source of the problem. A story of one man with multiple therapists illustrates this point.

Gene, a gay man who suffered from chronic migraines, was referred to an out-patient psychiatric clinic for short-term treatment because his health clinic could find no organic basis for the headaches. During the six weeks he saw the social worker, Gene was questioned about the sources of stress in his life. It turned out that he was a bank manager, very much in the closet, and had to listen to chronic anti-fag jokes without visibly reacting. The social worker concluded that his work was toxic and recommended he seek employment elsewhere.

After being discharged from the clinic, Gene still wanted therapy, so he started seeing a private practitioner. Although this therapist agreed that the job had something to do with his headaches, he also suspected a deeper cause. Gene's father, it emerged, also a banker, had never made it past branch manager. The therapist learned that Gene was slated for promotion to vice president at his bank. If he accepted it, he would have to deal with the guilt and anxiety provoked by surpassing his father in career achievement. It wasn't surprising, the therapist concluded, that Gene was having headaches. Together, they explored the historical causes for the client's fears about his father.

The difference between the first and second therapists' approaches was dramatic. Gene's headaches did not go away, however, until he went to a body therapist, who saw muscular tension as the source of physical symptoms and successfully used massage and breathing techniques to relieve Gene's stress.

It's Up to You

It should be clear from the foregoing that the array of differences — and choices — among therapists is enormous. It will be virtually impossible to discover, or to carve out, the therapist whose style, background, ethnic profile and fees match exactly what you want. You cannot draw up a chart and conclude, "I want a left-handed lesbian Lutheran who uses jargon sparingly, touches me often, never gives directions and perceives my problems in a nonhistorical way. Furthermore, she can never charge more than ten dollars a session and will be forgiving if I can't pay."

But the opposite of this overspecifying is just as unworkable. It means surrendering responsibility, trusting to blind luck, letting go of logic and intuition. It may reduce you — as it did one seeker of therapy — to judging a therapist's desirability by the location of her or his office and the length of time it took to find a parking space nearby.

The Power Imbalance

Added to the feeling of vulnerability built into the role of psychotherapy consumer, another obstacle may prevent consumers from specifying their preferences: therapists' resistance.

The power imbalance in therapy *is* real. The therapist is the sage professional; the client, the needy seeker. Because of this dynamic, your inquiries or assertions about what you want from therapy may seem presumptuous to the the therapist or to you. Because such assertions or questions challenge status quo, counselors confronted with such a challenge may not be pleased. Some therapists will be genuinely eager to share information. Others may be defensive; still others will feel it is their role to deflect questions, or to interpret their psychological meanings.

The author of another consumer's guide to therapy — a psychologist — describes his first meeting with a gay client in the following way: "The patient began his first session with an angry challenge. He said, 'Look, before I can tell you anything about what I've been through, I've got to know, what do you think of homosexuals?'" The author goes on to describe how he "disarmed" the patient of "his hostility" with a quip, and tells his readers (rather proudly) that he avoided answering the client's question with . . "an apologetic discourse on the plights and rights of homosexuals."

This therapist perceived a relevant question, undoubtedly posed with some urgency by the client, as hostile and unworthy of a serious response. Among therapists, such responses to clients' questions are not unusual.

As an empowered consumer, you are exploring new territory. Such an exploration deviates from the familiar script of an expert doctor "curing" the helpless patient. It may therefore be marked by self-doubt on your part and less than positive responses from your therapist.

You may doubt your ability to judge the therapist's competency. You may feel you have jeopardized therapy because you are unable to trust the therapist. The therapist may feel that you are cantankerous and resistant to therapy.

Bringing your own rating system to therapy is often accompanied by some discomfort. In addition to its quota of anxiety, however, such a departure from tradition may also have its benefits. By being aware of your own needs and goals as a consumer, you can multiply your chances of a genuinely helpful collaboration between counselor and client.

The basic theme of this book is that *as a consumer, you can affect what happens in therapy.* You can choose. You can express yourself. You can empower yourself. These decisions will be reflected in the whole shopping process. They will lead you to exercise power in the relationship. If your therapist is too directive and interventionist for your taste, say so out loud. After all, no one can be directive without a directee. If you're uncomfortable with the psychological jargon your therapist uses, you can say that you prefer everyday language because it's not so mystifying.

If, on the other hand, you wish to initiate *new* behaviors, there are also reasonable options within your grasp. For example, if you ask for a hug and your therapist is a formal, nontouching sort, you will probably get some facsimile of a hug. If you want to explore a childhood relationship that you feel bears on your present situation — even though your therapist is averse to such excavations — express your desire clearly. Your request will probably pay off.

Therapists, like most other people, operate within a range of behaviors and responses. Your own wishes will shape, within limits, the actions of the therapist. Saying, "I would like a hug," or "I would rather not be touched now," or "I feel undermined by your constant direction and advice," or "I'd like to know if you ever faced something like this in your life," are legitimate requests within the therapeutic setting.

Such requests will not always be easy to make. In fact, by the time they are easy you will probably be less dependent on your therapist. You may even be ready to leave for good. Nevertheless, they are requests worth making even when it is difficult to do so.

—9—
Negotiating Your Needs

Once you've decided to begin therapy with a counselor you've picked, how do you ensure that the process will meet your needs? The answer, in a word, is *negotiate*. It's never too late to express your desire to change an aspect of therapy. It's even better to establish certain ground rules from the start.

Payment Negotiations

Money is perhaps the most difficult area of negotiation in therapy. How can a price be assigned to caring and support? And if the caring and support are genuine, why must they be purchased? Often, therapists are no less troubled by this paradox than are clients.

Many therapists are sensitive and flexible about their payment policies. There are several steps to take which will place you at the lower, instead of the high end of the counselor's scale.

- If the therapist has been recommended by a friend, find out what your friend is paying and how the fee was determined. You'll have an idea about the therapist's approach and what he or she has charged in the past.

- Initiate the fee discussion at the beginning of the first call or the first session. A question like, "Do you have a sliding fee scale?" is a signal to the therapist that the fee is important to you, that your resources may be limited.

- If the therapist does have a sliding fee scale, and you feel you are an appropriate candidate for its lower end, be prepared to summarize your financial circumstances and any change you may anticipate. Therapists are more likely to give you a lower fee initially if it seems temporary.

- If the fee is fixed, or the scale too high, say that to the therapist and ask if it is possible to work something out. Some therapists are willing to exchange services. One woman, a gardener, took care of her therapist's lawn in exchange for therapy. Another woman supplemented the therapist's fee by making a quilt for her. To avoid misunderstandings in a bartering arrangement, it is advisable to assign a precise money value to the services you are offering. It is important to determine how many hours of *your* work at *your* rate equals the therapist's fee for service.

Bartering works well for some clients and counselors. Others report that such an arrangement interferes with therapy. A man who traded office work for counseling found that he could not respect his counselor after he saw how disorganized he was. A therapist had to discontinue a fence building exchange with a client because she was unable to let go of her counselor role and relax as she might have with a stranger. When the client showed up for work depressed, the therapist was tempted to offer her a "free" session.

With such sensitivity surrounding the issue of money, it is hard to evaluate therapy's cost realistically. Compounding the problem is the enormous variation in fees — which are not necessarily linked to the skill of the therapist. Fees are mostly a function of the type of license the practitioner has, the area of the country and the current demand for his or her services. Consumers who have weathered the fee-setting process deserve a respite from the tension that surrounds money matters. Unfortunately, fee setting is only the beginning of fiscal negotiations in therapy.

How the fee is paid also varies significantly. Some therapists prefer cash; some want checks. Some ask to be paid at each session; others prefer to bill to avoid dealing with the exchange of money during a session. If you are not clear about your preference, chances are the therapist's will prevail.

One woman reported coming out of the first session in a daze, realizing that she had just agreed to be billed every month. She most emphatically did *not* want to get a bill for two hundred dollars in the mail on the first, along with her mortgage, gas, electric, phone and credit card bills. Paying on a weekly basis would have been more workable fo her.

Another woman reported that two months after she began therapy and settled on a fee with her therapist, the therapist raised the fee by fifteen dollars. By that time the client had begun therapy in earnest and didn't feel like shopping anymore. Had she known such a raise was imminent, she would never have begun with the therapist. It's important to find out when the fee is set what the therapist's policy is about raising it in the future.

One man was very depressed after the death of a close friend, and called the therapist several times between sessions. At the end of the month, charges for the time spent on the phone were added to the bill. The client was furious. He had never been told that he would be charged for such mid-week tune-ups.

Therapists' policies in this regard vary. Therapists themselves may not be clear. They may apply different policies to different clients. One therapist charged a client who called him a lot and didn't charge another who called him less frequently.

Changes in circumstance can be another sensitive area. One psychologist could barely suppress his outrage when a client on the lowest paying end of his scale inherited a substantial sum of money and didn't suggest a fee increase. In fact, the client railed at length about the fair weather friends who were descending on him for a handout. The psychologist, angry as he was, nevertheless felt that mentioning the subject would make him appear to be one of this greedy pack. He kept quiet and was relieved when the client dropped out of therapy.

The same situation occurred in reverse when a client who was injured was unable to continue working. She particularly needed the support of therapy during her convalescence, but was unable to pay the counselor's fee. She was afraid to ask for a fee re-evaluation, feeling certain that it would be turned down and cause her even more despair. Instead, she stopped therapy.

Insurance introduces yet another variable into the fee negotiations. If your therapy is partially covered by health insurance, it must be decided if the therapist will be paid by you or the insurance company. Virtually every insurance form has provisions for making payment to either party.

It is in your interest to pay as little out of pocket as possible; the therapist, however, will want to get paid as quickly as possible. Insurance payments, after claims are submitted, often take several months to process. So the therapist would prefer that *you* be the one to wait for the insurance payment. However, many therapists are flexible about this. The issue may be resolved by your assertive statement at the beginning of negotiations: "I can afford therapy because of the insurance. I am able to pay my share of the bill. I don't have enough cash flow to pay the whole bill and wait for the insurance."

When insurance is an employment benefit, clients often elect to pay whole fees themselves, out of fear that disclosure of their treatment will circulate within their workplaces. In addition, the insurance forms require diagnoses. Who sees these diagnoses and under what circumstances remains unclear.

Where insurance is involved, invasion of privacy is a risk. You've got to weigh the risk against the financial advantages of using insurance coverage.

If you elect to use insurance, you can minimize the risk by discussing the diagnosis with the therapist before she or he submits the claim. You have the right to be informed of the diagnosis that's being applied to you. Some diagnoses are more stigmatizing than others; clients diagnosed as psychotic or having a personality disorder will be perceived by anyone who sees the diagnoses as being severely disturbed. Other diagnoses (such as those in the "Adjustment Disorder" or "Life Circumstance" categories) emphasize that the disturbance is temporary, or a natural response to trying circumstances. They are therefore much more benign. The advantages of such a diagnosis on a claim seen by your employer are obvious.

In this culture, money matters are surrounded by a set of rituals and taboos that are difficult to avoid. Complicating an already complex situation is the enormous variation in how and when and what therapists are paid. Because policies about money are so arbitrary and individual, it is particularly important for you to determine what your own needs are. What is a reasonable amount to pay for therapy? When is the best time to pay? How do you want to pay? How do you feel about the therapist's money policies?

You may end up paying more or less than you figured, or in a different way. Nevertheless, it is important to have your preferences accessible — in your mind, or on paper — when you begin the process of negotiating for what you want and need in the therapy situation.

Schedule and Structure Negotiations

As well as questions about payment, the therapist's policies about cancellations or missed appointments are important to settle in advance. Most therapists charge for first sessions; a few therapists consider the first session an "evaluation" session for both of you and do not charge for this discretionary hour. Still others do not charge for the first session if you decided you can't work together. If it seems like a good match, however, and the evaluation session turns out to be the first therapy session, the client will usually be charged for it.

Most therapists' stated policy is that they charge for appointments which are not cancelled twenty-four hours in advance. If there are extenuating circumstances — you had a flat on the freeway, or got fired ten minutes before your appointment — they don't often charge. There are exceptions, however. One woman was shocked to find herself billed for an appointment she had cancelled well in advance. One psychiatrist charged his client for sessions when he, the psychiatrist, was on vacation. In the more traditional therapies, one's slot is permanently reserved. Such a reservation may mean that the client is expected to pay for all sessions, regardless of the circumstances.

Equally important to clarify is the way the therapist handles emergencies. How and when can the therapist be reached? Obviously therapists are not eager to be awakened in the middle of the night, or interrupted during nonworking hours. Still, the reactions to such calls vary enormously. Some therapists actively encourage clients to use them this way; most discourage it. The therapist's policies on emergencies, and whether there is a fee for phone calls, is important information. Ask for it at the beginning.

Same Time Next Week and Alternate Rhythms. A woman who was struggling with suicidal impulses needed a therapy session every couple of days and telephone conversation another couple of times a week. One man who had been through several years of therapy only wanted occasional tune-ups.

Therapy frequency depends on several factors: how much you need and want it, how much it costs, and how much time you have. Unfortunately for the consumer, outweighing all these considerations is the therapist's schedule. If his or her schedule is arranged around regulars — people who come at the same hour every week — or dictated by agency requirements, the therapist may not be willing or able to dislocate it with alternate rhythms.

The first step is to determine what rhythm feels good to you. There is nothing sacred about a week between hourly sessions. You may prefer another interval.

One woman who prided herself on her self-sufficiency found the idea of therapy an affront to her sense of independence. She decided to ease in and told her therapist she wanted to come every two or three weeks at first.

In another instance the therapist suggested that a client come twice a week, instead of the one time he had been coming. The client wasn't comfortable with such an arrangement — it cost too much and he was too busy. He rejected the therapist's suggestion.

Saying what you want as a consumer may make the difference in scheduling; it may not. Nevertheless, it is important to determine your ideal rhythm, and ask for a schedule that coincides with it.

Another dimension of therapy is length. Friends who are perennial therapy clients may arouse in us emotions which fall somewhere between pity and contempt. Statistically, people who go to therapy for years and years are rare. Although there are people who stay in therapy for fifteen, twenty, even thirty years, other people see a therapist only once. The average number of visits — if we count all the people who see therapists — is under ten.

This is another area where it is important to give yourself plenty of latitude. One woman reported that things really cleared up for her after one session. And one man says he expects to be in and out of therapy all his life. Just as there is no single reason for going to therapy, or single approach, there is no one correct length of time for remaining in treatment.

The Structure of Sessions. Initial contacts, first impressions, and fee policies all present opportunities to take stock, to measure and evaluate therapy. Several other factors lend shape to the therapeutic exchange. One is the structure or composition of the therapy session.

Greatly slowed video tapes of therapy sessions (or any human encounters for that matter) show sequences of finely-tuned exchanges — exchanges in which gestures and expressions as well as words are unconsciously synchronized. In slow motion, the interactions are so rhythmic as to seem almost choreographed.

One man, commenting on the process, said, "Sometimes therapy seems like a dance. . . or some kind of painting. . . but the palette is made of words and silences, movements and tone."

The particular composition of the first session may or may not be pleasing to you. One man dropped out of therapy because he thought the therapist talked too much. He felt undermined, as though the therapist thought he wasn't capable of coming up with his own answers.

In contrast, another man reported a need to be "warmed up." Too much silence immobilized him. He plunged deeply into thought without resolution, and ended in a negative spiral. He needed the therapist to structure the session actively, verbally and physically — it was important for him that the therapist leaned toward him and smiled at him from time to time. He used such structure to order his life both during the session and afterward.

Session Endings. After six months in therapy, Luke had resolved a lot of the questions he entered therapy to answer. One question remained unanswered, however. How, he wondered, did his therapist know, without seeming to look at a clock, that the sessions were over?

There are as many styles of ending sessions as there are approaches to therapy. Some therapists just seem to glide gracefully and effortlessly to the end of sessions. Other clients report a lack of grace around session endings. One woman reported that her therapist had a beep-alarm which went off precisely on the hour. It didn't matter if she was in the middle of sentence — the session was over. She began to end sessions herself in order to avoid being cut off.

One client's therapist had two clocks. One was placed

in such a way that the therapist could see it; the other was visible to the client. For this particular client, such an arrangement made the session endings seem less abrupt. Another client reported that her therapist never ended sessions when she was in the middle of a thought. Consequently, she often went overtime. It was lovely, she said, when the therapist gave her more time. The trade-off was the time she spent in the waiting room when her therapist went overtime with the client before her.

Session endings are another facet of session structure which provides an opportunity to monitor your own needs in the therapy process. Does the therapist's ending style feel comfortable? If not, how could it be improved?

A client who felt jarred by the therapist's ending style asked the therapist to guide her back to the present time before the session ended — particularly if she were talking about the past, painful events. The therapist agreed and the new arrangement made the client much more relaxed about exploring such difficult areas.

It's important to define the arrangement of words, silences, structured and unstructured time, and pacing of sessions that works best for you. Acknowledging your needs to yourself is the first step. It's legitimate to tell your therapist, "I need more structure dealing with this stuff," or "I would like you to put the clock where I can see it."

The therapist may or may not respond to your needs. What matters most is that by making the request, you have affirmed that your needs are important. In short, you have asserted that *you exist* in the therapy situation.

Physical Impressions. The furniture in the room, its arrangement, the pictures on the wall, where you sit in relation to the therapist — all of these physical details contribute to your rapidly growing fund of impressions and feelings. One woman reported that she felt physically far away from her therapist when she wasn't getting her point across, and closer when she felt understood, even though their chairs never changed position.

One man said he spent most of the first session silently trying to forgive his therapist for having such execrable baroque taste in furniture. He had to struggle with himself to be open-minded enough to make another appointment. When he went back for the second session, they met in a different office — simply and sparsely furnished, and much more to the client's taste. It turned out that someone else had been using the therapist's regular office the first session, and he'd borrowed an unused office for that hour.

Physical arrangements may provide the first opportunity to try out a self-empowered stance in therapy. One man who felt too far away from the therapist thought, at first, it would be presumptuous to mention it. Several sessions later, he took the cushions out of the chair he had been using and sat on them, using the chair as a backrest. Because he didn't get any flak from the therapist, the following session he moved the whole chair closer before he sat in it.

Another woman who was unable to talk much during the first half of the session because she was so overcome by grief, moved in mid-session to another chair. She thought that by leaving her sorrowful self symbolically in the first chair, she could begin to talk.

Tuning in to your physical needs isn't limited to seating arrangements. One therapist ran a space-heater too high to suit a client. After several minutes of dialogue with herself, a client went over and lowered it. Another person who was distracted by noise from the street asked her therapist to shut the window.

We have all learned early that it's rude to go to someone's house and start rearranging things. And we've learned to be particularly respectful in the offices of professionals. Adopting a consumer stance toward psychotherapy means accepting another view. Everyone has preferences: certain temperatures, lighting, and seating arrangements feel better than others. When we walk into a professional's office, we automaticaly shelve such preferences. We are so accustomed to our powerlessness in such situations that we may not even be aware that the chair is too hard or the light too bright. After all, why allow ourselves to be aware of such discomfort if we can't do anything about it?

You may or may not opt to *do* anything about your discomfort. But paying selective attention to it will help attune you to the sensations you're experiencing. How does the chair feel? The distance from the therapist? The temperature? The light? The noise?

If you find that the office light is too bright, or the street noise distracting, and you mention it, you give the therapist (and yourself) more than information about your discomfort. Encoded in your statement is a second message: *My needs are significant in the therapy situation.*

"I exist" seems like a simple enough statement. It

seems obvious and easy. Yet we make the opposite statement — "I don't exist" — automatically when we don't
tune into our needs. Our silence says it for us.

A Therapy Contract: Is It for You?

Approaching a first interview with a checklist is a
radical departure from traditional procedures. An even
more radical departure is preparing a contract. Recommended by a consumer protection group in 1975 as something for therapists to provide, the idea has not been wel-
comed by the profession; nor is it likely to be. It can,
however, be a valuable tool for consumers.

A contract may specify only the mechanics of treatment, or it may include goals. It may be written, dated
and signed or it may be just an oral agreement. In its most
informal form, it can be simply a verbal statement of
goals, and a mutual agreement to review the goals with a
specified time frame.

What reaction can you expect when you broach the
idea of a contract? Chances are the therapist, accustomed
to directing the course of therapy without interference,
may be unenthusiastic if you produce a contract. And it
will be easy for the therapist to turn a perceived infringe-
ment on her or his turf into some unfavorable perceptions
of the client — a perception that you are defensive or resistant to therapy.

Plenty of consumers don't like contracts either,
feeling that they are too binding. One woman said she
went to therapy to be surprised. Though interviewing the
therapist seemed fine to her, the notion of a contract
seemed to rob the exchange of its potential spontaneity.

Another woman said the need for a contract dissipated after she brought it up in the first session, and the therapist seemed quite open to the idea. The therapist's attitude was reassuring enough to make a contract unnecessary.

Here is an example of a more formal written approach:

CONTRACT

Dennis Tai agrees to join with Jeff Hirsh every Thursday for one hour for a three-month period from October 4 to January 3, at 3 p.m. Such an arrangement is subject to change at any time by both parties if a 24-hour notice is given. During these 12 sessions, we will direct our mutual efforts toward two goals:

Enabling me to understand and alter the sources of my excessive anxiety in social situations.

Enabling me to deal with my feelings toward the long illness of my father.

I agree to pay my share — $25 per session — which will be supplemented by insurance payments of $25 per session paid directly to Jeff.

If at any time during the sessions, I feel I am not satisfied, I can cancel the remaining sessions. If Jeff feels that further work with him is not advisable, he can discontinue the sessions. At the end of the 12 sessions, Jeff and I agree to renegotiate this contract. We include the possibility that the stated goals will have changed during the 12 session period. I understand that this agreement does not guarantee that I will have attained these goals;

however, it does constitute an offer on my part to pay Jeff for access to his resources as a therapist in good faith.

I further stipulate that this agreement become a part of the record which is accessible to both parties at will, but to no other person without my written consent. The therapist will respect my right to maintain the confidentiality of any information communicated by me to the therapist during the course of therapy.

I do not give Jeff permission to publish, communicate or otherwise disclose without my written consent any information which pertains to me or these sessions.

Signed by Dennis Tai   Jeff Hirsh   Oct. 4, 1984

The contract is only an agreement and not necessarily a legally binding document. But it can give consumers a sense of order and control over the therapy process. It *does* represent acknowledgement of a collaboration between clients and therapists.

Useful as it is in this regard, the contract has its limits. As a predictor of what will actually happen, the contract won't suffice. Despite the precision with which one outlines goals and the steps toward their achievement, no one can foresee and limit the course of therapy. And contracts, written at the beginning of therapy, may turn very quickly into fossils — interesting, but useful only insofar as they record a past reality.

─10─
Therapist/Client Interactions:
The Hazards of the Journey

It is futile to generalize about the many facets of the therapist/client relationship. There are so many possible differences in arrangements, needs, styles, and approaches that such a generalization would be superficial. But there are some dynamics which are too common and too powerful to be omitted from this guide. Emotions like dependency, anger, eroticism, and boredom can transform a civilized therapy session into a wild trek through uncharted territory.

During the course of therapy, clients often experience feelings towards their therapists that are so intense they threaten to disrupt the process. But the very emotions which endanger the therapy relationship can be transformed so they become the moving force that drives it forward.

Dependency

"I feel like I can't wipe myself without my shrink."

For adults accustomed to coping with jobs, freeway commutes, and complex relationships, it can be a devastating realization. Kansas said, "It hit me when my therapist said she was going on vacation for three weeks. Three weeks without talking to Nancy? Impossible. Unthinkable." On the way home she got angry. She thought it was outrageous that Nancy had been so casual. She'd gotten her hooked. Now, Kansas thought, it's *her* responsibility to take care of me.

Who doesn't want to be self-sufficient? Increasing one's self-reliance is often the very reason people have sought counseling in the first place. Consequently, it may come as a shock to feel that you *need* your therapist.

A counselor can play a unique role in our lives; one that is likely to generate feelings of dependency. Different therapists relate to dependency feelings in different ways. Some encourage clients to air and analyze those feelings, particularly if they are frightening; they believe that in doing so, clients provide valuable information about themselves.

In some therapy situations, dependency may never be mentioned aloud. Perhaps such feelings are uncomfortable to both client and therapist; tacitly they agree not to acknowledge them. Therapists who favor a problem-solving, or behavioral approach may see such feelings as being outside the scope of their focus.

The way dependency is dealt with in therapy depends on the self-awareness and the orientation of both client and therapist. Regardless of your therapist's approach, it is probably worth it for you to delve into these feelings. They often provide insight about your relationships both in and outside of the therapy office.

Greg came to therapy to examine his feelings about intimacy. He'd realized that he made it a point to juggle several lovers at once, while remaining equally distant from all of them. When he realized he was postponing decisions until his therapy session, Greg was horrified. The feelings he had been maneuvering to avoid were coming up in relation to his therapist. His urge was to bolt, to get out of therapy so he could reassure himself that he was indeed in charge of his life.

Fear of dependency is pure common sense. Everyone has learned, probably starting in the crib, to limit reliance on other people. Who hasn't been disappointed by parents, friends, lovers? And your therapist will probably disappoint you at some point, too. But the therapy relationship offers you an opportunity, a place slightly safer than most, to look at your feelings and the ways that they shape all your relationships. The therapy situation also gives you an opportunity to see how many of your fears are realistic and how many are outmoded responses, leftovers from a time when you really did have fewer resources than you do now.

Anger

At some point you'll probably get angry at your therapist. Every relationship includes a certain amount of toe-treading; therapist/client relationships are not exempt. Some therapeutic schools maintain that a client's irritation at his or her therapist reflects unexpressed feelings toward parents or other significant people. Other therapy approaches take client anger at face value: You're really angry at the therapist for the reason you state.

Disagreements about money and time probably prompt most of the anger clients feel. One therapist raised her fee five dollars every year. A client she had been seeing for several years says that she could count on being furious every January when she had to change the figure on the check.

Another therapist frequently ran overtime. After going a few minutes over with six or seven clients in a row, he was often a half hour late by the end of the day. A client whose work schedule required him to take the last appointment was chronically angry. The fourth time it happened, he just walked out of the office.

Unwanted comments from the therapist can also trigger angry feelings. One woman who was seeing a straight therapist was infuriated when the therapist suggested that her chronic feelings of inadequacy might stem from regret that she wasn't a man. As a feminist and a lesbian, the client found this interpretation unacceptable and insulting.

Angry feelings mixed with guilt are an even more unwieldy combination. One man was irate when he arrived for a session and found a note cancelling his appointment. His anger turned to guilt when he found out that the therapist was ill and had been taken to the hospital. Now he felt guilty. It seemed an impossible situation for him. How could he be angry when she was ill?

Even if you manage to weather your anger and bring it

up in a therapy session, there's no guarantee that you'll be satisfied with your therapist's response. He or she may be defensive, apologetic, reassuring, understanding or neutral. Expressing angry feelings toward your therapist may feel like throwing darts into cotton candy.

It's not easy to talk about anger. Unexpressed anger probably accounts for more disenchanted therapy consumers than anything else.

"Nothing really happened," or "It was just a waste of time and money," are comments that come up frequently in the conversations of dissatisfied consumers. Probe a little deeper, and what generally comes out is unexpressed anger: an episode, a comment, a minor dissatisfaction which the client didn't voice. Unspoken anger turns into numbness and obliterates every other feeling. Then, it becomes true that nothing *is* happening.

For clients who express anger during a session, there's usually a positive postscript. The therapy relationship has been tested and risked. If it lasts, it's stronger. Knowing that you can get angry, that the anger subsides without anybody collapsing, and that therapy can continue, affirms the strength of the relationship at least as much as any exchange of warmth between client and therapist.

Sexual Attraction

Falling in love with your therapist: how boring, how trite. It's as bad as falling in love with your gym teacher — and most clients go out of their way to avoid it.

One man was certain he'd protected himself. He'd made sure to choose a counselor who was not his physical type. Nevertheless, during the second session he found himself in the middle of a very detailed sexual fantasy about the therapist.

Cliches contain a core of truth. Passionate feelings for one's therapist are pretty common. They may be even more difficult to weather than dependency or anger, and they may go hand in hand with both. There may be agonizing weeks or months where the therapist's smallest gesture of support raises hopes of reciprocal feelings.

Sky was so attracted to Cecile, her therapist, that she drove by her house frequently, hoping to catch a glimpse. She called Cecile late at night and hung up when she answered. After three months of this (all of which remained unknown to Cecile), Sky decided that her feelings were hopeless and she stopped therapy.

It isn't surprising that erotic feelings develop in therapy. Researchers who have done studies about interpersonal attraction have isolated several factors which lead to passion. We are likely to get turned on to people who arouse positive feelings in us. And, we tend to feel close to people we have regular contact with. The therapy relationship meets both criteria: the therapist is supportive and warm; the contact is regular and ongoing. And the therapist may know more of your secrets and inner thoughts than anyone else — even your lover. If the therapist is lesbian or gay, you might even encounter her/him in bars, at meetings, gay events. Consequently the chances for more informal interaction are increased.

If the pain of unrequited love for your therapist is unbearable, it's time to consider your options. Many clients and ex-clients claim that working through such feelings can be a valuable part of the therapy process. On the other hand, you may feel that your focus on the counselor obstructs the work you're in therapy to do. If the impasse seems unresolvable, you may be tempted to drop out. Before you make a final decision, take a break. The intense feelings may subside when you're away from direct contact with the object of your love. If they do, reevaluate the situation. If they don't — and you're convinced that no amount of time will help — look for other support. A group may be useful if you're reluctant to seek out another counselor.

If, on the other hand, your therapist initiates sex with *you*, there is only one course of action: stop therapy immediately. A therapist who violates the legal and ethical sanctions against having sex with clients will not provide a therapeutic environment for you. If several months have elapsed since the end of the therapy relationship, sexual conduct with your ex-counselor no longer violates any formal code of professional conduct. Nevertheless, the dangers of such encounters are great. When you and your counselor exchange your confidante/advisor role for a sexual partnership, questions about exploitation and betrayed trust are bound to arise. These doubts, as well as your original inequality, may make a post-therapy relationship difficult to maintain — and even more difficult to let go of. Finally, it is unlikely that your future choices about therapy can be neutral or free from the fear that you — you and your new therapist — won't be able to stay on course.

Sex with a therapist, even an ex-therapist, can be psychologically harmful; it can, in fact, reinforce the problems that first caused you to seek counseling. Even when the emotional consequences are not serious, such encounters further complicate the already complex business of seeking and evaluating therapy and therapists. As a therapy consumer, your most valuable tool is your own judgment. Keep it objective.

Boredom

If you feel bored in therapy, chances are that what you're *not* saying is more important than what you *are* saying. As illuminating as the content of your secrets may be, it's often the *process* of secret-keeping that's most significant. Your most authentic self has taken a hike, and left an imposter who only pretends to be talking about something meaningful. It doesn't feel right.

LaDene reported feeling muffled in dullness during her sessions. She was afraid she'd fall asleep. She started drinking coffee before her appointments, to no avail. LaDene wanted to tell her therapist about her boredom, but was afraid she would hurt the therapist's feelings. She realized she had been "sparing" the therapist this way — keeping her own feelings under cover for months. This, LaDene knew, was her pattern outside of therapy as well. When she finally discussed her fears in a session, she cried. She felt present for the first time in months.

In long-term therapy, the significance of boredom is worthy of exploration. It may reveal some unspoken reluctance to continue the therapy process — a way of shutting down to ward off painful thoughts and feelings. It may signify the client's readiness to terminate therapy, even before that sense of completion has been verbalized by client or therapist. Or, it may indicate the reaching of a plateau, the kick-off point to the next level of insight.

Like other feelings that emerge in therapy, boredom often carries information which is relevant both to therapy, and to outside relationships.

Unendings; 50 Ways (not) to Leave Your Shrink

The one thing it may be possible to generalize about is how hard all endings are. Saying goodbye is usually a painful experience for humans. Therapy endings are no exception. Neither therapists nor clients want to experience the losses, abandonment, and deaths that are part of life.

In actual practice, there are ways around goodbye in the therapy relationship. It's not necessary to say goodbye. "I'll come back when I need you," or "I'll check in from time to time," or "I just need some time off to integrate what's been going on," are all good ways of avoiding a permanent goodbye.

Therapists' versions of unendings may look slightly different. In *The Effective Psychotherapist*, (1982), author David Brenner writes: "Intentionally, the termination visit has not been discussed in any detail in this book. When used in the context of an effective helping relationship, the word termination has an inappropriate finality to it."

A strong aversion to "the end" may originate in feelings that business has not been finished. Perhaps therapists believe they haven't done enough — they feel guilty. And clients who don't believe they have shared all the negative feelings they have don't feel "finished" either. Or, perhaps ending is the most difficult juncture in therapy because it is the one with the fewest positive precedents. Most of us don't feel good about loss, abandonment, and death — our most common models for separation.

Seth had been through a series of deaths before he was old enough to feel much except helplessness. His mother died when he was two and his grandmother died two years later. His father died of cancer when he was twelve. The thought of ending therapy brought up all the old feelings, bad dreams, and middle-of-the-night bouts with terror about his own death.

Seth rehearsed his leave-taking with the therapist months before he left. He imagined what the final session would be like, the final walk down the stairs in front of the therapist's office, the final stepping off the curb in front of the therapist's building.

Despite all the rehearsal, the grief Seth actually experienced was strong enough to send him back to the therapist's office two days later. He continued therapy for another four months. When he left for good, he felt he had achieved the first separation in his life which left him and the other person intact and strong. Nevertheless, he felt sad about the loss for almost a year.

When One Is Not Enough

Some clients come to therapy to get help resolving a clearly identified issue in their lives. Others come because they are overwhelmed by an array of feelings they hope to sort out and deal with. In either case, it may be most useful to see more than one therapist — simultaneously or sequentially. The therapist who's doing a great job helping you resolve your anger at your father may not be the best person to see about your sexual problems. The recovered alcoholic who's supporting you through your withdrawal from drinking may have no experience dealing with your incest experience. Seeing a series of therapists over a period of years is, in fact, the norm for many clients. Unfortunately it is also the norm to view this phenomenon as a "failure" of therapy. If therapy had been successful, the argument goes, why would a second or a third therapist have been consulted? The successful therapy experience, according to this argument, entails a finite course of treatment with one therapist, who deals effectively with every aspect of the client's situation.

The recognition and acknowledgement of a multiple-therapist approach to treatment is long overdue. Asserting the right to define for ourselves what "successful" therapy means to each of us is one more step towards consumer empowerment.

Is There Life After Therapy?

In one study, 82 percent of clients who had just finished a satisfying course of treatment couldn't say they had no further need for therapy. It's no wonder that a frequent criticism leveled at therapy is that cures get submerged in an overwhelming tide of dependency which is fostered by the therapy process itself.

Specific endpoints in therapy may be illusory; most therapy clients will continue to go regularly or sporadically.

One graduate student, guilty and anxious about his gay feelings, confided in his program advisor. The advisor recommended a sympathetic counselor, and the student spent the next two years in therapy, coming out and establishing a circle of gay friends. Soon after he was ensconced with a lover, the client decided he was through with therapy. He thought he had come a remarkable distance and felt very positive about the experience.

Two years later, when he and his lover were breaking up, he returned to the same therapist — this time for six months. Again he felt supported. Within the next ten years, therapy-free periods of several years alternated with times — usually periods of several months — when he went back to his therapist.

Most people enter therapy during times of crisis. Therapy may not continue, but life and its periodic crises do. If you had a positive experience the first time around (and in some cases, even if you didn't), you are likely to gravitate again towards a known source of support. There may not be life after therapy. It is probably more realistic to say that therapy is a continuous, if episodic, part of many of our lives. The probability of repeated returns to therapy underscores the need for clients to develop a strong consumer orientation from the start. Such an assertive approach will ensure positive therapy encores instead of a futile search for the one counselor or therapy technique which will finally "work."

You and Your Ex

"Certainly there is a statute of limitations on professional relationships and one day we shall be friends," wrote a woman to her therapist when she left therapy.

Many lesbian and gay consumers choose straight therapists, or go out of town to avoid touchy situations that arise when therapists and clients come from the same community. Such situations become even more ambiguous after therapy is over. You and the person you worked with are no longer client and therapist to each other. If you are both gay, you are more likely to share a social network. Whether or not to ask your ex-therapist to dance when you run into each other at a bar or party has yet to be decided by the arbiters of gay etiquette. And what if you do dance, what then?

One therapist ran into an ex-client at a workshop almost a year after they had stopped therapy. They paired up in a couple of the workshop exercises and got together for coffee a few times afterward. Even though they joked about their old roles, they both felt awkward. Eventually they both acknowledged that they couldn't undo their history together and gave up.

A genuine transition from a therapy relationship to a friendship is possible, but not probable. Still, warm post-therapy feelings between counselor and client are an indication of a mutually positive therapy experience.

——11——
Handling Impasses
in Therapy

Many therapists will label anything the client does which interferes with the therapy process as resistance. If you hesitate in your choice of therapists, or question the therapist's interpretations or competency, or drop out of therapy, you may be labelled as a resistant client.

According to the psychoanalysts who first identified "resistance," clients who are anxious about the possible emergence of threatening unconscious material — their dreams, wishes, thoughts — will try to avoid their appearance. Clients will stop therapy, accuse their therapists of wrong-doing — anything to avoid the pain of self-knowledge. Overcoming client resistance is the perennial subject of psychologists' training seminars; no therapist or counselor-to-be can escape articles and lectures which focus on the subject. To many therapists, client resistance is a clinical entity — as real as torts are to lawyers or bacteria to physicians.

The resistance theory places the consumer with a complaint in an indefensible position. It is hard to feel legitimate, to leave or change what is happening in therapy, when your complaints are dismissed as "resistance."

Some of your complaints about therapy may indeed come from such resistance. Other grievances, however, legitimately arise from the current relationship between you and your therapist.

Ways around Impasses

Vic went to Dr. Bardini, a psychiatrist, because he was afraid to drive on freeways. His job, 45 minutes away by freeway, took twice that long to get to by the alternate route he used.

Vic and Dr. Bardini explored his early experiences, reasons he might be angry enough to go out of control, jump a divider and have a head-on collision with an oncoming car. They talked about his present fear of being dependent on his lover. Vic had insights galore, but he continued to use the frontage road to get to work.

Discouraged after six months of therapy, Vic said that he was ready to throw in the towel. Dr. Bardini insisted that the first step of Vic's recovery would be his ability to tolerate the continued closeness of the therapy relationship even though it was not providing him with gratification. When he could surrender that intimacy, Dr. Bardini stated, the freeway driving would take care of itself. Six months later, Vic was still in therapy and spending three hours a day getting to work and back. And he still couldn't get Dr. Bardini to acknowledge that therapy wasn't working.

Did Vic have a legitimate complaint? Did he have any options? Is it realistic to expect a "cure?" Whose responsibility is it if there is not even the slightest improvement in the problem?

Every professional group has ethical rules that guide its practice. Because these rules are good reference points during impasses in therapy, it's useful to know which practices fall inside ethical boundaries, and which do not. Ethical principles for counselors and other mental health professions are similar to The Ethical Principles of Psychologists which are summarized below:

- Psychologists recognize and acknowledge the limits of their knowledge and experience. In situations where their knowledge or experience is exceeded by the severity of the problems, they disqualify themselves.
- They recognize and respect differences of race, gender, ethnic, socioeconomic backgrounds and make sure that they have training adequate to provide competent service to the members of these groups.
- They recognize that personal problems can interfere with their effectiveness and refrain from any activity where such problems might harm a client.
- They reveal information about clients only with the written consent of clients or in those cases where danger to the client or others may result.

• They avoid exploiting the trust of clients. The most obvious instance, clearly unethical, of such exploitation, is sex between client and therapist.
• They avoid any situation which might result in conflict of interest and potentially impair professional judgment.
• They contribute a portion of their services to work for which they receive little or no financial return.
• They terminate a therapeutic relationship when it is reasonably clear that the consumer is not benefiting from it. They offer to help the consumer locate alternate sources of assistance.

Perhaps Dr. Bardini was unaware of the limits of his own competence. Perhaps he refused to admit that Vic was not benefiting from therapy. In any case, he did not opt to end the therapy relationship and help Vic find an alternative. Having failed in his direct appeal, Vic terminated his treatment. But there is a better alternative for such an impasse.

Getting a Second Opinion

It is so common for medical practitioners to get another professional's opinion that most insurance policies cover an outside consultation fee. Therapists often follow the same procedure. When they are stuck in a treatment impasse with clients, they frequently consult a colleague.

Sometimes you, as the client, may want to get a second opinion. You may seek the new perspective that consultation with another therapist can offer; you may see it as a useful adjunct to current therapy. What reaction can you expect to such a request?

The first therapist may be antagonized. The second therapist, the one being consulted, may be suspicious. Are you avoiding an important juncture with your original therapist? Are you acting out some archetypal triangle? It is difficult for you to defend yourself against such murky and contradictory motives. Group consultation — where you, therapist and the consultant are present — is one way to avoid the charge that the consumer is somehow circumventing the treatment process by going to someone else.

A straight therapist who was working with a gay man agreed with the client's request that it might be useful to have a session with a gay therapist present. The client knew no gay men and was in the process of coming out. The gay therapist shared some of his experiences and gay resources with the client and with the straight therapist.

In another situation, a third person was called in to mediate a dispute between a client and counselor — a long-brewing controversy over the payment of fees. The client and counselor were both active members of the lesbian feminist community in a California city. The counselor knew that the client was active in various women's projects but had very limited income. Consequently, she charged the client her lowest fee, $15 a session, and did not press her when she missed a payment.

The counselor's anger was triggered when her client departed on an expensive vacation. The counselor began to press the client for payment of the bill which now totalled several hundred dollars. The client resented this perceived inconsistency and felt she had been abandoned after their long history together. She announced that the bill was the counselor's problem, not hers, and refused to settle it.

As this impasse went on unresolved, both agreed to consult a third party: a woman in the community who did agency mediations. The mediator listened to both the counselor and client's account of the history of their relationship, and did a step-by-step examination of each person's feelings along the way. During the session the counselor took responsibility for the guilt she felt about charging any fee at all to a client who was doing such important community work. She admitted that this guilt had eventually turned into anger. The client acknowledged that, because she and the counselor were almost friends and shared the same interests, she resented paying for therapy at all. This had led her to tolerate an accumulating bill and expect free therapy.

During the meeting, which lasted over two hours, the two women renegotiated their client/therapist contract. They decided to keep working together and to review regularly all money issues between them. Both agreed that it would be important, in order to avoid all similar money dilemmas in the future, for the client to pay at each session. She agreed to pay off the outstanding bill in fifteen dollar a month installments.

A group consultation may not seem as threatening to your therapist as a separate consultation undertaken outside of her/his presence. It can, however, be threatening in another way. In a mediation such as the one described above, the therapist forfeits his or her helping role. The therapist in this new situation is, to some degree, a client. Many counselors may not choose to abdicate their authority in the interests of a negotiated solution.

Also, new issues arise from the situation: the fee of the mediator, and whether the original therapist will charge for the mediation session. In the situation described above, the therapist did not charge the client for the session and they agreed to share the fee for the mediator. There is no formula for this, and although some therapists may agree to such a consultation, they may not agree to share the cost of the mediator, or to consider the mediation session a goodwill contribution. In such cases, a third party mediation can be too expensive to consider.

If you and your therapist have reached an impassse, his or her reaction to a proposal that you bring in a third party will depend on the prevailing philosophy of treatment. Therapists who favor an egalitarian relationship, particularly feminist and gay-affirming therapists, are more likely to accept such a proposal. This is one more good reason to seek such a therapist in the first place.

Formal Grievance Procedures

Unfortunately for psychotherapy clients, no one has much to say about what goes on in therapy sessions unless a client gets beaten, molested or bilked out of a family inheritance.

Lesser breaches of the Ethical Code (e.g. not knowing one's limits, or not referring a client to a more appropriate counselor) are not taken very seriously by therapists, clients or their communities. Even in those cases which are reported, retribution may consist of nothing more than a mild rebuke from a professional association — if it occurs at all. Physicians who make comparable errors of judgment may well face a malpractice suit. But a therapist can give bad advice, make inaccurate interpretations, and cause much grief without fear of being challenged, sued, or censored.

What can the consumer do about this? How can you protect yourself?

Frustrated psychotherapy consumers have access to a series of very underutilized procedures for processing grievances. These procedures require self-assurance, and a large measure of conviction about their legitimacy. Despite the efforts of many therapists to foster their clients' self-determination, they have not encouraged this sense of legitimacy when it comes to questioning psychotherapeutic methods or techniques. Such validation, it appears, *will not* come from practitioners in the field of psychotherapy. It is not in their interest to transform a group of unquestioning clients into consumers who view their therapeutic experience with a critical eye. Such steps must be taken by consumers who are informed enough, and have the overview it takes, to empower themselves to act.

Watchdog Organizations. Consumers have several options for redressing violations of psychotherapy ethics. Local mental health associations, usually listed in the phone book under Mental Health Association of ----- County, represent one complaint route. These citizen-run watchdog organizations consider it their business to deal with instances of client abuse.

The National Association to Prevent Psychotherapy Abuse also focuses on the problems of psychotherapy consumers. This organization offers everything from moral support to attorneys' names.

There are other avenues for aggrieved psychotherapy consumers. Licensed therapists, or interns or assistants who are supervised by licensed therapists, have received their permits to practice from a state licensing board. This board will respond to consumer complaints submitted in writing. Investigations of the complaints may involve hearings with both parties present, and occasionally site visits. After the investigation, the board can make a recommendation that the charges be dropped, or that some penalty be imposed. Penalties range from admonishment to the revocation of the therapist's license to practice psychotherapy.

In this process, the ethical committee of the practitioner's professional organization is usually notified, and if the complaint against the professional is substantiated, this organization, too, can impose a penalty — either a rebuke or dismissal from membership.

Procedures for initiating such actions vary from state to state. If you want to have a complaint investigated, you must use the specific procedural channels of your locale. To find the name and telephone number of an individual state licensing board, call the state capitol building and request the number of the office which issues licenses for psychotherapists.

If the therapist is employed by an agency, there are complaint avenues within that organization. One can complain to any level of administration: the therapist's supervisor; the clinic administrator; the source of funding for the clinic; a private foundation; the Department of Public Welfare, and so on. If the therapist is licensed, the professional organization and licensing boards mentioned above are also avenues of possible grievance redress.

If the idea of pursuing such a course is too intimidating, there is the third party option. If you have a friend who is undaunted by institutions (it's particularly useful to choose someone whose work has justified the acquisition of some impressive letterhead stationery), such a person can file a complaint for you. It is perfectly legitimate for someone else to initiate any of the actions mentioned above on your behalf.

Legal Redress. Bad judgment on the therapist's part, or inferior treatment (as was true in Vic's case) are not grounds for legal action. A therapist, to be vulnerable to a lawsuit, must be shown to have significantly departed from the performance standards recognized by the profession — to have been negligent — or to have intentionally injured a client because of unprofessional conduct. Such conduct includes the disclosure of confidential information, physical assault, or sexual relations between therapist and client.

In 1976, a lesbian sued a psychiatrist who pressured her into sexual intercourse with him as a "cure" for "psychosexual" problems. Though she obtained a $25,000 settlement, the psychiatrist is still practicing in New York. He is also a contributor to an anthology on psychotherapy in which he explains a particular approach called Paradigmatic Psychotherapy. Published well after his trial, the book contains his description of the role of therapist which, presumably, is not intended to be ironic. The therapist, he says, should be a model for identification. "He . . . acts as a paradigm in the world, in which the patient must learn to move and to survive."

The psychiatrist is not only still practicing, but is also well-reputed enough in some larger community of therapists to be called upon as an expert in his particular area of therapy.

Sex between client and therapist is not an isolated phenomenon. Fifteen precent of the psychiatrists polled in a study done ten years ago acknowledged erotic behavior with clients. Five percent reported intercourse. Of this group 80 percent had had intercourse with more than one client, and in most cases intercourse was repeated. Though these figures represent pairings between male therapists and female clients, gay client/therapist relationships are not exempt. Among the more than 200 sexual contact cases reported in a midwestern clinic, there were eight cases of male/male involvement and 20 cases of female/female involvement.

Legal redress is an option for clients who feel they have sustained damages as a result of psychotherapy. This avenue is costly and time-consuming. The fact that psychotherapists pay a fraction of the malpractice costs required of physicians indicates that therapists don't run much risk of being successfully sued. Should you wish to follow the legal route, however, some addresses for gay and lesbian legal rights groups are listed in the Resource Section.

Therapists have a variety of approaches and techniques — all of which can be quite mystifying to the consumer. The tools listed here give psychotherapy clients some countervailing power. Even if you never use the procedures, just knowing they are available may give you a perspective that empowers you in a therapeutic setting.

III

Therapy
in Perspective

——12——
Mental Health for Lesbians and Gay Men

As members of a devalued minority, lesbians and gay men must contend with the dominant culture's contempt, hostility, and — perhaps even more devastating — its denial of our existence.

Each of us creates our own strategies for dealing with the inimical environment we live in. Some of us come out and some adjust to secrecy; some of us try to live in an exclusively lesbian and gay world and some of us shun that world.

Our collective experience has proven that what works best for us is not adherence to any one particular strategy, but rather the development of as broad a repertoire as possible. For some of us, at some time in our lives, psychotherapy is a useful part of that repertoire. But even the most positive therapy experience is just a supplement to the many strategies we employ daily, often unconsciously. It's tricky business, living congruently and comfortably as a member of two incompatible cultures — a minority and a dominant. Knowing what strategies have worked for other lesbians and gay men can help each of us develop even wider survival repertoires.

Coping Strategies

Coming Out/Staying In

Dear Tracy,

I've had a while to think about your letter and think it fair now that I tell you how I feel. If as you say you don't like men then I would respect your choosing to be celibate, but this immoral life you've inflicted upon yourself is obscene. You must now live in a narrow world because most people feel as I and your dad do. You will never be respected by anyone, only tolerated. You have chosen to live in a separate community that most people snicker at. You are making yourself a dirty joke. I'm sure you have rationalized your behavior by telling yourself this was born into you or acquired when you were young. To this I say *baloney*.

We are all complex human beings full of confusion and mixed feelings. It is important that we live by a standard that we respect. We must all be responsible for our actions and never be ashamed of what we do or what we are. If you are not ashamed of yourself I am amazed. I cannot believe that I could raise someone without a conscience.

You had the potential to be a force for good
in this very troubled world, and chose to join
the degradation. Our sorrow is overwhelming.

Mom

Tracy's mother's reaction to her daughter's self-disclosure illustrates why the question of coming out versus being closeted is one of the most controversial in today's gay and lesbian communities. Each side claims its strategy makes more sense. In fact, however, it is rare to find someone who abides solely in one camp or the other. The most upfront activists often have someone in their lives they don't tell; most closeted lesbians and gay men are out to some people. And there are very good reasons for both positions.

The decision to come out does not immunize lesbians and gays against the stress suffered by those who are closeted. Eric Rofes, in *Lesbians, Gay Men and Suicide*, writes:

"Perhaps no myth is so dangerous to lesbians and gay men as the myth that claims that the act of "coming out" as a gay person provides a person with a margin of insurance against self-hatred or self-destructiveness. This myth leads many lesbians and gay men to believe that, once able to be open about their homosexuality, their personal problems and anxieties will all fall by the wayside."

Examination of the advantages and disadvantages of both positions points to the wisdom of a nonprescriptive strategy. What seems to work best are decisions about disclosure which spring comfortably out of particular relationships and situations.

Work Strategies. In a recent study of lesbians and gay men who worked in corporations, the majority said most of their coworkers did not know they were gay. They felt such a revelation would jeopardize their jobs, their relations with coworkers, and their chances for promotion. Though they felt concealment was necessary for their protection, it caused them great stress. In contrast, a group of gay and lesbian community leaders, recently surveyed, attributed their professional and personal success to the fact that they were openly gay. Most of them, however, were self-employed professionals who had gay clients and collaborated with other gays in their professional and personal lives.

It makes sense. Being surrounded by people who reflect and affirm your lifestyle makes you feel good. Unfortunately, the vast majority of us are sequestered in organizations that are emphatically not gay-affirmative. To minimize the stress of working under these conditions, we need to develop coping strategies as reflected in the following examples:

A "headhunter" in an urban area compiled a directory of local corporations especially for his gay clients. It ranked these corporations by the level and pervasiveness of homophobia within them. Using this guide, local gays were able to concentrate their job hunts on companies which offered minimal stress to gay employees. Once ensconced in their positions, they could create an even safer environment by networking and building professional support groups, both inside and outside their organizations.

A teacher in a private fundamentalist school was extremely frustrated by the conservative atmosphere in which she found herself. She had to defend herself constantly to parents who accused her of not introducing enough religious material into her classroom. Under the guise of meeting the parents' demands, she convinced the administrator that the school needed a special curriculum for girls. She managed to get a special stipend for the project and persuaded the administrator that some of the time she now spent supervising study hall would be better used to do research for the new project. She spent these freed hours attending two womens' studies conferences, browsing through womens' bookstores, and meeting with feminist educators. The project was, for her, an antidote to the frustration she felt in her job setting.

A gay systems analyst had refused for years to accept a promotion because he feared such an advance would spotlight his gayness. Frustrated by the rut he was in, he teamed up with a lesbian programmer; they spent evenings and weekends together working on a software package. When they were close to finishing the project and had several nibbles from interested customers, they quit their jobs and went to work marketing the product. They used the proceeds of its sale to start their own educational software company. Although they had no more opportunities to work with gays than they'd had at work, they felt free of the closet. As independent contractors, they were less vulnerable to homophobia.

Two women administrators of a retail chain store invited the career-oriented lesbians they knew to an informal meeting for a discussion of work issues. The meeting created the nucleus of a lesbian career group which began meeting regularly. The group grew steadily; it provided the women in it with a forum for socializing and exchanging information about jobs and services.

Overcompensating on the Job: A Word of Warning

Overcompensation is a trap that lesbians and gays, like members of other devalued minorities, may fall into. Hoping to earn the respect of those who reject our life-styles, and attain some precious job security, we may work harder and longer than our heterosexual coworkers. But even recognition as "good workers" won't gain us admission to the social network that exists at most work-places. The "old boy" mentality is well intact in today's business world. Successful lawyers, executives, trade unionists and insurance salespeople share hobbies, church pews, and barstools. They belong to the same clubs and have similar requisite nuclear families. Such af-filiations are critical to their professional success.

No matter how diligent we are, as gay men and les-bians, we have no access to acceptance that is based on social conformity. Lesbians, especially — who face the double jeopardy of being both gay and female — are un-likely to fit easily into the average workplace "scene." Overcompensation, while doing little if anything for our careers, can have disastrous effects on our self-esteem. It makes it hard for us to recognize the isolation and victimi-zation we face from hostile coworkers and employers. It makes it easy for us to perceive denied promotions and fir-ings as personal failures.

Relationship Strategies

We are building our own personal, custom-made support systems. Because they look so different from heterosexual nuclear families, however, we may not recognize them.

Charles went to Otis, a counselor, complaining about being lonely. He couldn't seem to find his one and only, the ideal man with whom he wanted to settle down forever. When Otis questioned him about his current living arrangement, he beamed. He said he had two roommates, and that he loved both of them. They'd lived together for years and had known each other for years before that. They ate together, occasionally slept together, and one or the other was always available to go to a movie or a bar. When Otis suggested he might have already found his ideal "mate," Charles was amazed.

We have created alternative families. We may call them roommates; they may be ex-lovers who we're still closer to than we are to our current heartthrobs. They may be children we have elected to have as single parents, or collectively with the help of several non-biological parents. There is an infinite number of combinations that refuse to be tortured into some semblance of dominant culture nuclear families.

Relationships, like workplaces, are tempting arenas for overcompensation. We try to be "good" by having long-lasting marriages that replicate those our parents had, or strove to have. Maybe we muse that, if we do everything they did, we'll be acceptable.

But this strategy has a fatal flaw. Lesbian and gay relationships are without the social glue that helps keep heterosexual marriages together. Social acceptance, extended biological families, and the exemplars of marriage that fill TV and movie screens provide no support for lesbians and gay men.

What we *do* have is our *own* social glue — the source of which, ironically, is our membership in a stigmatized group. It is sticky enough to bond people of every conceivable variation in class, race, political persuasion. Because the glue is so unique, the affiliations it holds together are also different from relationships in the dominant culture. We have reason to respect and be proud of our relationships in all their nonconformist, freeform shapes. That is the key to our self-affirmation.

Sources of Lesbian and Gay Affirmation

The Lesbian and Gay Culture. "I've probably been to a hundred women's concerts. I always swear I won't go to another one. I've memorized all the performers' songs and raps. But the strange thing is I keep getting high from them over and over again. Just going into that auditorium with all those women. . . It's electrifying; when I leave I always feel like I've gotten my batteries recharged. Usually I didn't even know they were run down."

We live in two worlds. It's difficult to carve a self-affirming niche out of the straight world. But it's the other world we live in that reflects our reality. It is a world of gay and lesbian books, plays and music. It's full of places where we can meet and engage each other. It's made up of people who are astonishingly diverse. It includes groups in which we meet to talk about our lives, to get sober, to read poetry, to share childcare.

Our world is not as large as the bigger world we inhabit — but it's wide and far-reaching. There are sources of gay journals, hundreds of gay and lesbian organizations, businesses and meeting places sprinkled across the country. This network is largely underground — yet it's accessible to anyone who cares to find it. Although this network circles the globe, it is much underutilized. Only a fraction of the men and women who have chosen same-sex partners have ever participated in a lesbian or gay rap group or read a gay publication.

Members of most minority groups can identify and draw strength from their heritages. But we have a hard time locating our gay cultural histories. Unconnected to our roots, we are particularly vulnerable to a culture that finds us abhorrent — if it recognizes us at all.

Yet we are forced to spend most of our time in that unfriendly culture. We go to work, buy groceries, take buses, go to restaurants and movies — all the while taking it for granted that we will be chronically misperceived and misrepresented in these settings.

Although we haven't inherited a strong cultural identity, we have created one. This niche we have carved for ourselves offers us more than acceptance for choosing a same-sex lover. By participating actively in its growth, we help inoculate ourselves against the toxic projections of the dominant culture.

Social Action. One gay counselor reports that he's noticed two things that invariably — and quickly — interrupt a client's downward spiral. "Not necessarily in this order," he says, "they are: a new lover and a new cause."

Many lesbians and gay men corroborate his belief in the benefits of participating in social activism. A gay man says, "Talking about injustice wasn't enough. I had to find an outlet for my anger — and that was political action. My gay men's group shared a common understanding of gay oppression and we wanted to do something about it. So we started writing down all our experiences. Then we turned them into a script and started performing our play at a readers' theatre. We're presenting material that says we are okay... that we believe in accepting differences in sexual preference, or color, or age, or size, or physical ability. It's been a tremendous experience for all of us."

Many avenues of social action are open to us as lesbians and gay men. The communications explosion has resulted in the exposure of previously hidden information — information that social movements can use to change public opinion. We know when there's a chemical spill in the Midwest, a coup in Latin America, a black woman elected mayor of a small Southern town, or a test of some new nuclear weapon.

Becoming politically active is a strategy with a double payoff for us. We enhance our own mental health by externalizing and focusing the anger we feel. And we build bridges to groups and individuals that are fighting for the kinds of social change that will benefit us. By connecting in positive ways with people who are not gay, we counteract both our own feelings of isolation, and the homophobia that flourishes in the world around us.

As lesbians and gay men, we have developed a wide range of strategies to help us cope with the obstacles we encounter in our lives. Psychotherapy is one coping strategy among many. It is not the most common way of getting help. If there were a map a mile high and a mile wide that represented all the ways people take care of themselves, therapy would be a tiny dot on it. Talking to friends, being with lovers, crying and laughing, thinking and playing, working, traveling, sleeping, jogging, spiritual pursuits, the passage of time and plain old ingenuity are all alternatives to psychotherapy. When they result in more self-acceptance — when they lessen the toxic effects of living in a homophobic culture — they are the real "cures" for the problems we face.

Gay Liberation has written a new agenda for mental health. It has fostered the growth of alternative resources, including gay-affirmative psychotherapists, rap groups, resource people, and counseling centers. It has laid the groundwork for the creation of spin-off chapters especially for lesbians and gay men in already existing national organizations, such as Alcoholics Anonymous and Al-Anon. It has highlighted the entrenched homophobia in the mental health field.

But the most important contribution of our liberation movement is the growing awareness it has brought to each of us about the insidious effects of homophobia in our lives. That awareness has helped us learn to judge ourselves by our own, relevant standards, and to reject the inapplicable values of the larger culture. It has strengthened our collective demand for mental health services that accept us for who we are, and that help us follow the unique and elegant rhythms of our own lives.

—IV—
Resource Section

Resources

Tear-Out Shopping List and Sample Contract;
Gay and Lesbian Organizations, Directories,
and Non-Urban Networks

Tear-Out Shopping List
Questions to ask a possible therapist

Attitudes
Have you worked with lesbian/gay clients? _____
What has your experience been?

_____
_____
_____

How do you feel about a lesbian or gay orientation?

_____
_____
_____

Have your attitudes changed? _____
How? _____

_____

From your point of view, what causes sexual orientation?

_____

_____

_____

Training and Experience
What is your training and experience? License?

_____

_____

_____

What is your approach or theoretical orientation?

_____

_____

_____

Money
What is your fee? _____ Do you have a sliding fee
scale? _____ If so, what is your scale? _____
_____ Do you charge for the first session? _____
Can I count on this fee as long as I am in therapy with
you? _____ If not, what can I expect? _____
_____ When? _____
I want to pay (once a week, once a month, by cash, by
check, by insurance). Is my preference acceptable to you?
_____. What are your policies about cancel-
lations? Emergencies? Phone calls? Insurance diagnoses?

_____

_____

_____

Evaluation
After hearing about my reasons for coming, what are your

impressions?

_____

_____

_____

How do you see us proceeding? _____
Now? _____

_____

Future directions? _____

_____

Other comments? _____

_____

_____

Tear-Out Sample Contract

_____ agrees to join with _____
each _____ from _____ to _____ at
_____. During these sessions, each
lasting _____ minutes, we will direct our efforts
toward the following goals:

_____

_____

_____

I agree to pay _____ per session for the use of
_____'s resources, training, and
experience as a therapist. This amount payable _____

_____.

If I am not satisfied with the progress made on these goals,

I may cancel any future appointments by giving _____ notice, or _____. If I miss a session without _____ forewarning, I am financially responsible for that missed session, exceptions to this arrangement being unforseen and unavoidable accident or illness.

At the end of _____ sessions, _____ _____ and I agree to renegotiate this contract. We include the possibility that the stated goals will have changed during the _____ period. I understand that this agreement does not guarantee that I will have attained these goals; however, it does constitute an offer on my part to pay _____ for access to her/his resources as a therapist and her/his acceptance to apply all those resources as a therapist in good faith.

I further stipulate that this agreement become a part of the record which is accessible to either party at will, but to no other person without my written consent. The therapist will respect my right to maintain the confidentiality of any information communicated by me to the therapist during the course of therapy. I give/do not give my permission to _____ to audiotape sessions for her/his review. However, s/he will not publish, communicate or otherwise disclose without my written consent any information which pertains to me.

_____   _____
Client's Signature   Therapist's Signature
Date _____

Gay and Lesbian Organizations

American Association of Sex Educators, Counselors and
    Therapists, Gay, Lesbian and Bisexual Caucus, Box
    834, Linden Hall, NY 11354

American Mental Health Counselor's Associates, Gay/
    Lesbian Task Force, c/o Moon Valley Counseling Asso-
    ciation, 502 E. Tam-O-Shanter Drive, Phoenix, AZ
    85022

American Psychiatric Association, Caucus of Gay,
    Lesbian and Bisexual Members, c/o Stuart Nichols, Jr.,
    245 East 17 St., New York, NY 10003

American Psychiatric Association, Committee on Gay,
    Lesbian and Bisexual Issues, 1400 K St., NW, Washing-
    ton, DC 20005

American Psychological Association, Committee on Gay
    Concerns, 1200 17 St., NW, Washington, DC 20036

Association of Gay and Lesbian Social Workers, c/o S.E.
    Cor. 6th and League Sts. (1041 S. 6 Street), Philadelphia,
    PA 19147

Association of Lesbian and Gay Psychologists, 210 Fifth
    Ave., New York, NY 10010

Caucus of Social Work Educators Concerned with Gay
    and Lesbian Issues, c/o James Kelly, 5675 Spreading
    Oak Dr., Los Angeles, CA 90068

Institute for the Protection of Lesbian and Gay Youth, 112
    East 23 St., New York, NY 10025

National Association of Alcoholism Counselors; Gay
    Caucus, c/o Tom Rooney, 4210 South 36 St., Arlington,
    VA 22206

National Association of Gay Alcoholism Professionals —

Connecticut Chapter, PO Box 8871, New Haven, CT
06532

National Association of Social Workers Committee on
Lesbian and Gay Issues, 7981 Eastern Ave., Silver
Springs, MD 20910

National Caucus of Black Gays; Black Health Professionals of NCBG, 930 F St. NW, Washington, DC 20004

National Council on Social Work Education; Task Force
on Gay/Lesbian Issues, c/o Susan I. Frankel, 490 West
End Ave., #3-B, New York, NY 10024

Gay and Lesbian Directories

As well as providing regularly updated lists of bars and
other lesbian and gay meetings places, the following
guides include the names and addresses of counseling
centers, switchboards and other mental health resources
for lesbians and gay men.

Gaia's Guide by Sandy Horn. Send $10.00 to New Earth
Feminist Books and Records, 2 West 39 Street, Kansas
City, Missouri 64111.

Places of Interest 1984; *Gay Guide with Maps — USA and
Canada*. Send $10.00 to Ferrari Publications; PO Box
35575, Phoenix, AZ 85069.

Places of Interest to Women. Send $9.95 to Ferrari
Publications, PO Box 35575, Phoenix, AZ 85069.

Gayellow Pages. Send $10.00 to Renaissance House, Box
292WW, Village Station, New York, NY 10014.

The National Gay Health Directory. Send $3.95 to the
National Gay Health Coalition Educational Foundation, 80 S. Elliott Pl., Brooklyn, NY 11217.

These guides can also be ordered through Lambda Rising. For a copy of their catalog, write to Lambda Rising, *The Whole Gay Catalog*, 2012 S Street NW, Washington, DC 20009.

National Networks for Lesbians and Gay Men without Access to Urban Resources

A complete list, which includes local as well as national publications, is included in most of the guides listed above.

R.F.D.: A Gay Country Journal for People Everywhere
    Route 1; Box 127-E
    Bakersville, N.C. 28705
The Wishing Well
    PO Box 117;
    Novato, CA 94948-0117
Lesbian Connection
    PO Box 117;
    E. Lansing, MI 48823
Journey (the publication of the Metropolitan Community
    Church, which has branches in many cities and offers
    outreach services to rural lesbians and gay men)
    5300 Santa Monica Blvd.
    #304
    Los Angeles, CA 90029

References

Chapter One
page

18 "Over half of the 5,000..." Jay, K. and Young, A., *The Gay Report*, 1977, p. 698.

18 "— In contrast with their..." Bell, A. and Weinberg, M., *Homosexualities: A Study of Diversity among Men and Women*, 1978, p. 440.

18 "— 24 percent of black homosexual men..." *Homosexualities*, p. 450.

18 "White lesbians and gays..." *Homosexualities*, p. 450.
"Approximately 30 percent..." Saghir, M., and Robins,

18 E., *Male and Female Homosexuality*, 1973: reference cited in *Lesbians, Gay Men and Suicide*, Rofes, E., 1983, p. 74.

18 "Almost twice as many..." *Homosexualities*, p. 460.

18 Freud, S., *A General Introduction to Psychoanalysis*, 1924, p. 420.

20 Jung, C.G., *The Collected Works of C.G. Jung*, Volume 10, 1964, p. 107.

20 Berne, E., *What Do You Say after You Say Hello*, 1972, p. 351.

21 "The majority of Americans..." San Francisco *Chronicle*, November 9, 1982.

21 Steiner, C., "Times Are A' Changin'" in *Men Against Sexism*, ed. Snodgrass, J., 1977, p. 165.

21 "A recent survey of..." McDonald, G., "Misrepresentation, Liberalism and Heterosexual Bias in Introductory Psychology Textbooks," *Journal of Homosexuality*, 1981, #6, (3).

22 "In one such experiment..." Emond, N., "The Consequences of the Lesbian Label on Social Workers' Judgments of the Lesbian," Unpublished Doctoral Dissertation, 1979; Levi, T., "The Lesbian: As Perceived by Mental Health Workers," Unpublished Doctoral Dissertation, 1979. Lipinski, M., "The Effects of Client Gender, Client Sexual Preference and Therapist Gender on Client Prognosis," Unpublished Doctoral Dissertation, 1979.

23 Steiner, C., "Times Are A' Changin'" in *Men against Sexism*, Ed., Snodgrass, J., 1977, p. 164.

24 For a discussion of Lesbian/Gay Affirmative Therapy, see Clark, D., *Loving Someone Gay*, 1977.

Chapter Two
page

27 For a historical perspective of the "treatment" of homosexuality, see Katz, J., *Gay American History*, 1976, p. 129-207.

28 Tripp, C.A., *The Homosexual Matrix*, 1975, p. 237.

29-40 The stories of Edward and H. are taken from Katz, J., *Gay American History*, 1976. The unattributed stories are from personal interviews.

32 Broverman, I., et al., "Sex-Role Stereotypes and Clinical Judgments of Mental Health," *Journal of Consulting and Clinical Psychology* 34, No. 1, 1970.

36 For a discussion of Radical Therapy, see Agel, J., Ed., *The Radical Therapist*, 1971 or Wyckhoff, H., Ed., *Love, Therapy and Politics*, 1976. For a discussion of Feminist Therapy, see Robson, E. and Edwards, G., *Getting Help: A Woman's Guide to Therapy*, 1980; or Greenspan, M., *A New Approach to Women and Therapy*, 1983; or Robbins, J. and Josefowitz, Eds., *Women Changing Therapy: New Assessments, Values and Strategies in Feminist Therapy*, 1983.

Chapter Three

page

42 "Some would have..." Garfield, S. and Kurtz, R., "Clinical Psychologists in the 1970s." *American Psychologist*, 1976, 31, 1-9.

43 For a comprehensive review of available therapies, see Corey, G., *Theory and Practice of Counseling and Psychotherapy*, 1977; or Herink, R., Ed., *The Psychotherapy Handbook*, 1980.

54 "Forty-three percent..." Kiernan, T., *Shrinks, Etc.*, 1974, 250.

Chapter Five
page

86 "In one research study. . ." Strupp, H. and Hadley, S. "Specific Vs. Nonspecific Factors in Psychotherapy," *Archives of General Psychiatry*, 1979; and Rioch, M., Elkes, C., and Flint, A., *National Institute of Mental Health Project in Training Mental Health Counselors*, No. 1254, 1965.

Chapter Seven
page

113 "According to one research survey. . ." Hubble, M., and Gelso, C., "Effects of Counselor Attire in an Initial Interview," *Journal of Counseling Psychology*, 1978, 581-584.

Chapter Eight
page

122 Brenner, D., *The Effective Psychotherapist*, 1982, 41.

128 The quote "The patient begins his first session. . ." is from Amada, G., *A Guide to Psychotherapy*, 1983, 68.

Chapter Nine
page

135 For a discussion of diagnoses and their meanings, see Levy, R., *The New Language of Psychiatry*, 1982.

145 The contract is reprinted from Hare-Mustin, R., Maracek, J., Kaplan, A., and Nechama, L., "Rights of

Clients, Responsibilities of Therapists," *American Psychologist*, January 1979, No. 1, p. 8.

Chapter Ten
page

152 "Researchers who have done studies. . ." Bersheid, E. and Walster, E., *Interpersonal Attraction*, 1978.

155 Brenner, D., *The Effective Psychotherapist*, 1982, 103.

157 "In one study. . ." Strupp, H., et al., *Patients View Their Psychotherapy*, 1969, 75.

Chapter Eleven
page

162 The Ethical Principles of Psychologists appear in *American Psychologist*, June, 1981, 633-638.

166 For a discussion of ethical violations, see Hare-Mustin, R., et al., "Rights of Clients, Responsibilities of Therapists," *American Psychologist*, Jan., 1979; Sider, R., Ed., "Clinical Ethics in Psychiatry," *Psychiatric Annals*, April, 1983, Volume 13, No. 4; or Knapp, S., and Vandecreek, L., "Malpractice as a Regulator of Psychotherapy," *Psychotherapy: Theory, Research, and Practice*, Volume 18, No. 3, Fall, 81, 354-358.

169 "In 1976. . ." Bromberg, W., "The Perils of Psychiatry," *Psychiatric Annals*, 13:31, March, 83, 219.

170 "He . . . acts as a paradigm . . . " Herink, R., Ed., *The Psychotherapy Handbook*, 1980, 458.

170 "Sex between client. . ." Kardener, S., et al., "A

Survey of Physicians' Attitudes and Practices Regarding Erotic and Non-Erotic Contact with Patients," *American Journal of Psychiatry*, 1973, 130: 1077-1081.

Chapter Twelve
page
176   Rofes, E., *Lesbians, Gay Men and Suicide*, 1983, 49.

177   Hall, M., "In a recent study..." "Gays in Corporations: The Invisible Minority," Unpublished Doctoral Dissertation, 1981.

177   "In contrast..." Russo, A., "Finding the Gay Elite," Paper presented at 1981 American Psychological Association annual conference.

About the Author

Marny Hall, Ph.D., is a licensed psychotherapist. Throughout her ten years in private practice, she has worked with lesbians and gay men in groups, couples, and individual therapy. She is the author of several articles which have appeared in professional and lesbian publications and has contributed chapters to three anthologies. In 1980, Dr. Hall produced the videotape *Gays in Corporations*, which has been used both in gay and corporate settings. Dr. Hall is an active member of the San Francisco Bay Area lesbian community.

Charles Silverstein is author of *A Family Matter: A Parents' Guide to Homosexuality*, *Man to Man: Gay Couples in America*, and, with Edmund White, *The Joy of Gay Sex*. He is also the founding editor of *The Journal of Homosexuality*.